RENEW YOUR MIND, ENGAGE YOUR WORLD

ENCOUNTER
WITH GOD

AMAZING GRACE

250 years on, the beloved hymn continues to remind us that our destiny in Christ is secure throughout the storms of life.

LEVITICUS | HOSEA | LUKE | JAMES

JANUARY–MARCH 2023

Scripture Union

Thank you for buying *Encounter with God.*

We hope you'll find it a real blessing as you delve regularly into God's Word.

Scripture Union – beyond Bible reading guides

By purchasing this Bible reading guide, you are helping to support Scripture Union's mission to reach the next generation with the good news of Jesus. All profit made from the sales of this resource are used to introduce children and young people to Jesus in a whole range of exciting ways. Thank you for the part you're already playing in that.

Get further involved

If you'd like to find out more about Scripture Union, or you'd like to get further involved, go to **www.su.org.uk/beyondbibleguides**

About Scripture Union

Scripture Union is a Christian charity, inviting children and young people to explore the difference Jesus can make to the challenges and adventures of life.

Through a wide range of activities and initiatives, we provide opportunities for young people to explore the Bible, respond to Jesus and grow in faith. Having been established in England over 150 years ago, Scripture Union is now a global movement active in over 120 countries.

We believe every child should have the chance to discover Jesus. And, with an estimated 95% of children in England and Wales not part of a church, we're working harder than ever to take the good news of Jesus beyond the church in exciting and culturally relevant ways.

Scripture Union, Trinity House, Opal Court, Opal Drive, Fox Milne, Milton Keynes MK15 0DF, UK
Tel: 01908 856000 Email: info@scriptureunion.org.uk Website: www.scriptureunion.org.uk

Design by The Smithy Creative
Printed by Thomson Press, India

Lord of the Storm

Severe storm events are expected to be more frequent as our climate changes, but storms can also take other forms. After the pandemic, and acts of war in eastern Europe, the whole world feels storm-damaged. What can we do?

It was during a terrible storm at sea that John Newton reached out to God and came to Christ – his 'great turning day'. He set aside a conversion anniversary each year on 21 March to remember this salvation, both physical and spiritual. His famous hymn, 'Amazing Grace', was written 48 years later in 1773, when Newton was a 70-year-old clergyman. It may be based on a slave song heard in his brutal trading days. He preached a New Year's Day sermon on 1 Chronicles 17:16,17, and from his notes one can see that the phrasing and comments pre-empt the hymn's poignant words. This song has never gone out of use: it has been reimagined and updated and never fails to remind us that our destiny is secure.

Newton preached: 'You are entered upon a New Year. It may be your last.' This may not feel encouraging but it is realistic. We do not know when we will be called into the next life, and the uncertainty of global events can only underline the fragility of human wellbeing. Ultimate security is, however, ours. We can invest confidently in the kingdom of God and in our salvation through Christ alone. Jesus was right there in the boat with his disciples when the storm blew up, and Jesus was full of the power that overcame not just a storm, but death itself. We may feel that justice, peace and healing are slow to be revealed in this life, but the Lord's eternal justice, grace and love will confront us and heal us when we see him.

We enter today upon a new year. May we live it with a fresh commitment to Jesus and may this quarter's Bible notes bless us all. Newton's sermon included the line: 'Grace to any dear to us, peace in our families, his blessing with us a church and a people.' And also to you. Amen.

Sally Nelson
Editor

Annabel Moule
Content Assistant

ON THE COVER: **'It was during a terrible storm at sea that John Newton reached out to God and came to Christ.'**

Image credit: Shutterstock / Grodfoto

The Writers

 MIKE ARCHER is Vicar of Highfield Church, Southampton and has been working in parish ministry since 1994.

 EMMANUEL OLADIPO started as a Schools Worker in Nigeria, then served as the Africa Regional Secretary of SU and then as International Secretary. He now enjoys his retirement in Leicester together with Ruth, his wife of 51 years.

 AMY HOLE is serving her curacy at two churches in central Sheffield, and teaches Greek and biblical studies at St Hild College, Yorkshire.

 JAMYS CARTER is an Elim minister who now serves as a Focal Minister in St Polycarp's C of E in Sheffield. He continues to write and teach as the occasion arises.

 JOHN GRAYSTON is now retired after 37 years on the Scripture Union staff. John still writes, teaches and preaches, and he is on the leadership team at Tile Kiln Church in Chelmsford.

 JULIE ROBB leads the MA in Biblical Interpretation at London School of Theology. She also teaches on the Eastern Region Ministry Course and is an Adjunct member of Faculty for Samford University, USA. She is married to Tim, an Anglican vicar, and they have one daughter.

 TANYA FERDINANDUSZ from Sri Lanka is a freelance writer and editor, and has been writing Bible reading notes, articles and devotionals for over 20 years.

 KAR YONG LIM teaches New Testament studies at Seminari Theoloji Malaysia, Seremban, Malaysia. He is also an Anglican priest with the Diocese of West Malaysia.

 SALLY NELSON is the Dean of Baptist Formation at St Hild College, Yorkshire, UK, where she also teaches Christian doctrine and pastoral care. She is a Baptist minister and has been the commissioning editor for *Encounter with God* since 2015.

 ANNABEL MOULE is the content manager for *Encounter with God*. She studied English Literature at Oxford Brookes University and Theology at the University of Oxford.

Contents

Scripture Union is a member of the worldwide Scripture Union international community.
Website: https://scriptureunion.global

AMAZING GRACE IN 2023

It was John Newton's personal experience of God's goodness that led him to write 'Amazing Grace' – 250 years on, James Taylor also knows what it is to have been lost and found.

James grew up in Perranporth. His experience of God's wonderful love came through SU's Perranporth Mission. His parents were not Christians, but his mother used to take him to Perranporth Mission because he was an only child and she thought he'd enjoy playing with other children. James says, 'I went to the mission each summer from the age of three. When I was ten, the leaders gave me a youth Bible and a music tape by the Christian band Delirious?.'

> **I still remembered the kindness of the team, and that something about them was different.**

James kept the Bible by his bed but didn't reach for it, as he struggled with reading. But the Delirious? tape later proved to be a lifeline, as his life took a downward turn. James developed body dysmorphia, a mental health condition where he became obsessed with his appearance, which he felt was defective. By the time he was 11, he was starting to use drink and drugs as a means of escape. James did not go to the mission the following summer. He felt too disconnected from all it stood for.

Fast-forward to Summer 2001; James had turned 15 and was working at a local restaurant. 'A guy wearing a Perranporth Mission hoodie came in. We got talking, and I discovered that he was the Mission's leader! He invited me to come to the beach mission the following year. Previously, I'd only been to the beach mission because Mum took me, not because I was invited, but now, with a personal invite, I resolved to return. I still remembered the kindness of the team, and that something about them was different.

I once was lost and now am found

'The next summer, I went to the Mission, I asked loads of questions. But the real breakthrough came when a couple shared one evening how they had faced a really difficult situation and God had answered their prayers in a wonderful way.

'Afterwards, everyone went back to playing games and having fun, but I found myself unable to move from the table where I sat. I began to weep uncontrollably – I hid by flipping my hoodie over my head. I had been trying to carry so many things for so long, and suddenly I realised that despite the mistakes and wrong decisions I'd made, God forgave me. I accepted his forgiveness and felt his presence. His love entered into my heart, and he lifted all those burdens off my shoulders.

'As I wept, the Mission leaders would sit next to me and put their arm around me and show me that they were there for me. And as I peered up at other people through my teary eyes, I felt an overwhelming sense of love for them – a love so strong that if someone had asked, I would have died for them. And that's what set that experience apart from any other religion or faith, philosophy or idea, because I believe what I experienced was that sacrificial love for others that Jesus holds in his heart.

'That was my "born again" moment when I repented. I came out of the church feeling free and light. The Holy Spirit was working powerfully in my heart, and it was the start of the healing process for me. And from that time, having always struggled with reading, I was suddenly able to read my Bible, understand it, apply it, and it gave me life. That to me was nothing short of miraculous.'

Grace my fears relieved...

The next summer James was on the Mission's team. One evening, he had another incredible encounter with the Holy Spirit. 'I was hit by this amazing feeling of knowing I was totally accepted by God, just as I was. I felt whole and complete, filled with joy, utterly at peace and at one with myself. The body dysmorphia was gone, and I no longer felt self-conscious or any need to prove myself or compare myself to other people. I didn't know how to explain what was happening to me. It's like I got a glimpse of eternity.'

As John Newton expressed his faith experiences in song, James started expressing his in rap and poetry:

'I am a lion tamed by the Lamb,
holy and healing in God's hands, I am.
Safe on your wings, carry me you can.
Unfold your plan for the world to see,
let healing be. Put me on my knees,
the dark deceives, the animal in me breathes.
Let us all know new realities,
open the door, I want to be free like a bird that soars,
in you, I believe I'm a lion that roars.
From once touched now wanting more.
Hand of the lamb, heal this hurting land.
Let your love pour and let your stream of life explore.'

The Lord has promised good to me

A few years on, Perranporth Mission's leader invited James to do a church internship in the Midlands. Later, another friend from Perranporth Mission exhorted him to do an internship with DNA, a national organisation which equips people for church leadership. She helped to fund his placement, which was at her church in Essex.

From there, James spent two years on the house team and pastoral team at Lee Abbey, before completing a degree in theology at Trinity College in Bristol. More recently, he spent three years as a Methodist lay pastor in Cornwall, and in September 2021 he took up a post as minister of North Street Church in Taunton, his wife's home town.

'I'm loving being part of the church family here and leading it as we go forward. We have a congregation of about twenty on a Sunday morning, but we've just partnered with a local contemporary worship group and we've launched an evening gathering, focused on prayer and worship. Around fifty people are coming, some from other churches and some with no church connections at all. In the last few weeks several people have asked if they could be baptised.

'God has done fantastic things in my life. He's met all my needs. He's put me in a position where I'm able to feel fulfilled, and he's entrusted me with a huge responsibility of pastoring God's people. I can't really describe the level of gratitude I feel towards him. And I'm also so thankful to SU, the Perranporth Mission and those involved, because collectively they played a huge part in my discovering God's amazing grace for myself.'

At Scripture Union, we're passionate about seeing non-church children and young people like James discover a personal vibrant faith in Jesus. To find out more about our work, and to provide your support through your gifts and prayers or through volunteering at events like Perranporth, visit scriptureunion. org.uk. For more stories like this, subscribe to *Connecting You*, our free quarterly supporter magazine, at su.org.uk/connectingyou

mental
HEAL†H
and wellbeing

Mental health matters

Many children and young people struggle with their mental health. Perhaps more than you might think.

That's why we've developed a suite of *Mental Health and Wellbeing resources* to help children's and youth workers introduce the difference Jesus can make to the challenges of life.

Please pray that these resources will have a big impact and prove to be an invaluable tool for those working with struggling young people.

TO FIND OUT MORE OR TO ACCESS THE RESOURCES, VISIT SU.ORG.UK/ MENTALHEALTH

Using this Guide

Encounter with God is designed for thinking Christians who want to interpret and apply the Bible in a way that is relevant to the problems and issues of today's world. It is based on the NIV translation of the Bible, but can easily be used with any other version.

Each set of readings begins with an *Introduction* to the section you are about to study. The *Call to Worship* section at the start of each note should help you consciously to come into God's presence before you read the passage. The main *Explore* section aims to bring out the riches hidden in the text. The *Growing in Faith* section at the end suggests ways of applying the message to daily living.

The *Bible in a Year* readings at the foot of the page are for those who want this additional option.

Luke 14:1 – 19:27

CHOOSING THE KINGDOM

Just after Peter had confessed him to be the Messiah,[1] Jesus was transfigured by the Father and encouraged by conversation with Moses and Elijah to face the road ahead.[2] If anyone could identify with Jesus in this moment as they 'spoke about his departure, which he was about to bring to fulfilment at Jerusalem',[3] it was surely Moses and Elijah, who had also had to stand alone against impossible challenges. Encouraged and strengthened, Jesus was able to choose the kingdom.

Luke tells us that, after predicting his death a second time, Jesus 'resolutely set out for Jerusalem'.[4] From this moment on in Luke's Gospel, everything happens on that single journey to the cross.[5] Jesus has chosen the cross. Nothing and no one can deflect him from that purpose.

The kingdom that Jesus is choosing is a constant theme on the journey. Some of his listeners want to understand more about the kingdom – what it is and when it will come. Others oppose Jesus and scrutinise his every move. Some embrace the kingdom gladly, as an opportunity that might otherwise pass them by: the lepers, the blind and tax collectors. Others cannot bring themselves to do so or think they've no need of such a King. Everyone Jesus meets on the way to Jerusalem is challenged, by word, parable and deed, to choose the kingdom, to decide where their ultimate loyalty lies. Let us journey with Jesus as he walks towards Jerusalem and the cross. As he walks and teaches, let us once more choose Jesus as our King and embrace his kingdom.

Mike Archer

FOR FURTHER READING

Kenneth E Bailey, *Jesus Through Middle Eastern Eyes*, SPCK, 2008

Joel Green, *The Gospel of Luke* (New International Commentary on the New Testament), Eerdmans, 1997

John Nolland, *Luke*, Vol 35b and Vol 35c, Word Biblical Commentary, Thomas Nelson, 1993, 1994

---

[1] Luke 9:20 [2] Luke 9:28-33 [3] Luke 9:31 [4] Luke 9:51 [5] For other references see Luke 10:1,38; 13:22; 17:11; 18:31,35; 19:1,11

Stuck in the Middle

Reflect on key areas of your life this New Year's Day. Where are you hoping for change? Record your intentions and display them as your agenda for daily prayer.

In the middle of a story it's hard to trust God for how it will end. When, in the Second World War, the expeditionary force was stranded at Dunkirk, it was impossible to see a British Army returning to Europe to confront Nazi Germany. Despair was a reasonable response.

The writer of this psalm is disorientated; perhaps writing at the time of the Exile, when nation, king and Temple were all lost. Prayer is leading nowhere: feeling neither heard nor helped, seeking God leaves the writer sleepless, wordless and comfortless. The psalm reminds us how hard it can be to pray when stuck in the middle of a story. It reminds us that the Bible doesn't just contain God's Word to us but also our words to God, including bitter and despairing words. Though unanswered, this lament gives us clues as to how to wait for an answer.

In verses 10–13 the writer determines to remember what God has done, as a basis for believing that the despair he was feeling couldn't be the last word. The Exodus (vs 16–20) is still real, even in the midst of Exile, and there has to be a way forward even if it's as yet unperceived (v 19).

As I write for New Year's Day, this psalm is an uncomfortable one, but it reminds us that the experience of Exile was not God's final word. Nor will a pandemic be the final word, nor even a war in Europe. As Paul reminds us, God has kept all his promises in Jesus Christ.[1] Just as the psalmist remembered the Exile, so, for us, remembering Jesus, crucified and risen, helps us to respond in praise. However dark the middle of our stories might seem, we rest in the presence of the Lord, who will never leave us nor forsake us.

Despair has been closer to many of us over recent years. Alongside your agenda for prayer, record your reasons for thanksgiving and hope in God's promises.

[1] 2 Cor 1:20

BIBLE IN A YEAR: **Genesis 1,2; Matthew 1**

Luke 14:1–14

Invited and Set Up

Thank God for all your recent experiences of giving and receiving hospitality. How have they encouraged you? Perhaps make a point of thanking someone where they've encouraged you.

Jesus has been both invited and set up: a prominent Pharisee has invited him on a Sabbath and placed in front of him someone with an unmissable physical ailment (v 2). We're not told that the man has come asking for healing – and when he has been healed, Jesus sends him away (v 4), implying that he's not there as a guest, only as a trap. If Jesus chooses to heal, then it's unambiguously his choice. Everyone's watching to see what he will do.

The Pharisees refuse to answer Jesus' question about whether it's lawful to heal on the Sabbath. Even though it's something that only God can make possible, they refuse to engage with the question. Recognising the trap, Jesus steps boldly into it. After healing the man, Jesus simply asks how they would act in two urgent situations on a Sabbath. If it's right to act immediately to prevent harm, how can it be wrong to cure harm? Although they have no answer, they are not won over.

With the pre-dinner entertainment over, the guests are called through to dine. Watching the guests jockey for position, Jesus recommends humility: better to sit too far down and be called up than too high and get moved down. Now seated close enough to speak to his host (v 12), Jesus urges him to see hospitality differently: not as an exercise in politics, status and reciprocity, but as an opportunity to serve those who can never repay. The greatest reward, he suggests, comes to those who invite the poor and those in need. Serving someone like the man in the ante-room trap attracts the Father's blessing in a way that playing politics will never do.

Hospitality that reflects God's kingdom embraces the disadvantaged and the marginalised. In what ways can such hospitality be more fully expressed in your life?

BIBLE IN A YEAR: **Genesis 3,4; Matthew 2**

Feasting in the Kingdom

Pray for anyone you know at work or in your family who seems to be on the edges. Ask God to show you how to include them in community.

Jesus speaks this parable to reveal what feasting in the kingdom (v 15) really means. Two invitations were sent: the first a 'save the date', telling people when the event was planned; the second when the celebration was actually ready to go. Hence the servant's words in verse 17: 'Come, for everything is now ready'. Everyone to whom the servant goes had previously agreed to come to this celebration on this date. The excuses are flimsy. Nobody buys property without viewing it first – you have to check everything (especially the availability of water). Again, nobody makes such a massive investment as buying five pairs of oxen without first checking they can pull. The third guest doesn't even bother to be polite. He's so engrossed enjoying the pleasures of his honeymoon that he sees no need to apologise. Having previously agreed to come, they've now all refused.

The host had catered on the basis of the number who'd said they'd come. Everything will go to waste. So he reacts to their shocking rudeness by upending everything. Those recommended to his host by Jesus (v 13) are invited: the poor, the crippled, the blind and the lame. When they're within, the master sends the servant to those living in the roads and the hedges. These untouchables (in that culture) have to be firmly led into the banquet as they can't believe they're really wanted. Some argue that those in the town are Jewish people unable to keep the Law because of their occupations (like shepherds), while those in the roads and hedges outside the town are Gentiles. Those who received the 'save the date' refuse to come. That prompts the master to throw open the doors and invite everyone unable to keep the Law to feast at his table. That's what feasting in God's kingdom really means.

It's easy to exclude others unintentionally. Where that's happened to you, forgive: where you've done that to others, say sorry.

BIBLE IN A YEAR: **Genesis 5,6; Matthew 3**

Luke 14:25–35

The Road Ahead

Reflect on where following Jesus is costly at the moment. Ask for forgiveness and grace where you're struggling with that, and for fresh strength to keep going.

Having set his face towards Jerusalem,[1] Jesus is walking towards the cross. His choosing to walk the way of the cross is uncompromising. He will not – cannot – allow anything or anyone to stand in his way, as Peter found to his cost.[2] Turning to those who would walk this road with him, Jesus challenges them to reflect upon the cost of doing so.

It means, Jesus states, putting the kingdom before family. The hate is not literal, but it's a powerful way of stating that no other concerns can be allowed to register. Even the legitimate demands of family cannot stop us from pursuing the kingdom. Luke 9:57–62 captures three ways in which these demands are so powerful, constraining those who otherwise desired to follow. We cannot look back over our shoulders when we've started to plough, as that means we do nothing well. We have to make the kingdom the first and only priority. Without that clarity, his disciples cannot truly follow him. Walking this path with him, Jesus insists, means embracing suffering. Carrying a cross is burdensome, even if it's only the cross bar on our shoulders as Simon of Cyrene was forced to do for Jesus.[3] Jesus is clearly flagging up that this road is one that would be hard and likely to entail suffering. If they're not willing to embrace suffering, they should not follow after him as disciples.

What this amounts to, Jesus tells them, is counting the cost. If you can't complete a tower, don't start; if you can't resist an aggressor, sue for the best peace terms you can get. To paraphrase what Jesus says in verse 33, if they cannot wave goodbye to everything they have, they cannot be his disciples.

Joshua 24:15 captures the power of a family or household all pursuing God together. To what extent is that true for you and your household or community?

[1] Luke 9:51, KJV [2] Mark 8:33 [3] Luke 23:26

BIBLE IN A YEAR: **Genesis 7,8; Psalms 1,2**

Lost and Found

'... the joy of the LORD is your strength.'[1] Take some time to remember and give thanks for joyful times in your journey with God.

Jesus was under intense scrutiny. Yes, he ate with Pharisees, but he also ate with those they detested. Worse still, Jesus appears to have hosted them himself; he did not just accept their invitations (v 2). How could Jesus be holy, the Pharisees muttered, if he ate with those who were obviously not? Jesus answers them with the parables that follow. To the Pharisees, working as a shepherd meant you couldn't both do your job and keep the Sabbath. Being told to imagine themselves as sinners who have lost a sheep was challenging. (As a hundred sheep is too many for one person, the shepherd was probably responsible for a flock belonging to a community.) The sheep was probably missed just before they headed for home. Others took the flock back to the village (which is where the shepherd himself went in verse 6) while the shepherd went to seek the lost sheep. Separated from the flock, it was vulnerable. Perhaps walking in a wide perimeter around where the flock had been, the shepherd sought and found the sheep. Swinging it on his shoulders, he rejoiced because it was found. On his return, everyone gathered to rejoice that one of the community's flock had been found. Similarly, the woman didn't simply shrug her shoulders because she'd lost a silver coin. Investing time and energy to recover what was lost, she, too, rejoiced with her community when it was recovered.

The Pharisees are invited to understand that, like the shepherd and the woman, Jesus sees himself as responsible for seeking and finding those who are lost. That's why he rejoices – that's why heaven rejoices – when they're found. Jesus suggests, with real irony, that the Pharisees lack that joy of being found (v 7), because they haven't realised that they, too, are lost.

Pray for those you know for whom joy seems far away. Ask the Lord to strengthen them. Pray also for those who don't yet know they need to be found.

[1] Neh 8:10

BIBLE IN A YEAR: **Genesis 9–11; Matthew 4**

Luke 15:11–32

Prodigal Grace

Read Romans 8:15 and 16 aloud. Repeat it as though it's written just for you (eg 'by him I cry'). Ask the Spirit to embed these truths in you.

Sometimes naming something affects how we understand it. If we call this the parable of the lost son, which son do we mean? Both are lost, estranged from the father in different ways. The younger asks for his inheritance; the older does nothing to prevent this – and he also benefits.

We could also call it the parable of the prodigal father. First, astonishingly, he grants the younger son the means to repudiate him; next he runs to welcome the wastrel home. With ring, robe and calf, the father teaches us that we are to welcome, not despise, the younger son on his return (vs 22–25). That's what turns the self-interested calculation of verse 19 into the repentance that causes the returning prodigal to become a son again (v 21).

The most significant point is that the parable is left unfinished. While the first redemptive arc is complete, the second is paused, breathlessly, waiting to hear what the older brother will do. He humiliates his father by demanding a public confrontation (v 28). He denies their kinship ('this son of yours', v 30), exaggerates his brother's crimes ('prostitutes') and cannot rejoice that his brother has come home (young goat vs fatted calf, vs 29,30). Once again, the father shows extraordinary grace in going out to ask him to be reconciled to them both ('this brother of yours', v 32).

In leaving the parable unfinished, Jesus invites the Pharisees to see themselves as older brothers, unable to rejoice at the return home of sinners. Celebration is the only right response, something Jesus stresses through all three parables spoken in defence of his attitude to sinners. Jesus is asking the Pharisees, 'Will you also come home? Will you be reconciled to the Father who shows outrageous favour even to tax collectors and sinners?'

Reflect on the Father who runs to embrace the returning son. How deep has his love sunk into you? And is there anyone who needs the same grace from you?

BIBLE IN A YEAR: **Genesis 12,13; Matthew 5**

Faithful Risks

Remember how God was faithful through times when you've faced big decisions. Pray for any decisions you now face and for decisions faced by others known to you.

Accused of wasting his master's possessions, the steward faces ruin. Unable to dig and too proud to beg, he takes advantage of the hours left before he has to return the account books that symbolise his office. Summoning his master's debtors for private conversations, the steward radically reduces each one's debt, asking the debtor himself to make the amendment in the account book. As the steward had the right to act on behalf of his master, these transactions are binding. None of the debtors know that he is all but dismissed, so he uses his last hours in the job to create a reputation for his master of great generosity. The debts forgiven are huge: a large olive grove's annual produce or the rent of a farm twenty times larger than an ordinary family farm.[1] With the ethic of reciprocity fundamental to the culture, the steward will be treated hospitably everywhere he goes.

It's hard for the master to fight back. Demanding restitution would make him look foolish when currently he's loved for being generous. He's already dismissed the steward and can't pursue him for theft because he hasn't stolen anything, he's simply put money in other people's pockets. When the steward returns the account books amended by the debtors themselves, the master can only commend him for his shrewd opportunism. Jesus wants us to learn from the steward's shrewdness, not from his dishonesty. We're challenged to see wealth as a resource for the kingdom (v 9) and to give it away in the service of God to show that it is not our master (v 13).

The steward shows shrewdness to evaluate a situation and the courage to turn it to his advantage. Are there opportunities around you where a faithful risk might be God's call?

[1] John Nolland, *Luke* Vol 35b and Vol 35c, Word Biblical Commentary, Thomas Nelson, 1993, 1994

BIBLE IN A YEAR: **Genesis 14,15; Psalms 3,4**

Psalm 78:1–39

Purposeful Remembering

Paul tells us to present our requests to God with thanksgiving.[1] Spend time thanking God, perhaps writing those thanksgivings down or posting them where they can be seen.

Split over two Sundays, this psalm is unusual because, though written for public performance (vs 1,2), it is neither prayer nor praise. Its purpose is to instruct one generation so that it can pass on its faith to the next (vs 3–6). Of course, each of us has had the story of faith handed down to us by others, but here the purpose goes beyond learning to warning: to help future generations not just to remember past mistakes but to learn from them. Yes, future generations need to know 'the praiseworthy deeds of the LORD, his power, and the wonders he has done' (v 4), but they also need to learn not to become 'like their ancestors – a stubborn and rebellious generation, whose hearts were not loyal to God' (v 8). The psalmist wrote to help God's people break this repeating pattern (v 1).

During the national days of prayer called in the UK at the height of the Dunkirk crisis and the Battle of Britain, churches across the nation were full as people prayed for deliverance.[2] The six days after the first day of prayer saw unusually calm seas and 334,000 troops were rescued while Hitler unaccountably hesitated. I was ashamed that I knew nothing of this remarkable move of prayer and its results. After a pandemic in which the church initially locked its doors in the UK and in which our nation has not significantly turned to intercession, I feel rebuked that we have not learned from the past. The 'riddle' (v 2)[3] is: why do we behave as we do, knowing God to be as he is? And why does God behave as he does, knowing his people to be persistent in going their own way? Still he abounds in love and has to be driven to anger.

As your own purposeful remembering, record the past times and seasons when you've been particularly conscious of God's presence and his power at work.

---

[1] Phil 4:6 [2] RT Kendall, *Thanking God*, Hodder & Stoughton, 2003 [3] Eg New American Standard Bible; TNIV has 'lessons from the past', NIV has 'hidden things, things from of old'.

BIBLE IN A YEAR: **Genesis 16,17; Matthew 6**

A Named Person

Slowly and prayerfully, read Hebrews 13:5. Ask the Holy Spirit to show you how to trust God more in these key areas of life.

This parable challenges the Pharisees, who loved money and were sneering at Jesus just before our passage (vs 13,14). Lazarus, the only character in any parable named by Jesus, reminds us that even those most beaten up by life are named individuals, not just issues. Though later recognised by the rich man (v 24), no help comes his way. The dogs get the leftovers, not Lazarus. Those dogs are the only ones to show Lazarus compassion, for they lick his sores, a sign of canine affection which also aids healing.[1] In contrast, the unnamed rich man's lifestyle is one long banquet in the most expensive garments (even on the Sabbath).

After death, their fortunes are reversed. The rich man is in torment, outside looking in, whereas Lazarus, who had lain at his gate listening to daily revelry while starving to death, is now the guest of honour by Abraham's side. The rich man, however, is unabashed. He begs Abraham to send Lazarus to serve him in his torment, even though he'd not lifted a finger for the beggar when he was at his gate. Abraham explains that 'those who want to go from here to you cannot' (v 26). The next request is that Lazarus be sent to his brothers, but Abraham insists they have no need: they can learn all they need to know from Moses and the prophets. The rich man contradicts Abraham, insisting that they'll listen if someone comes back from the dead.

The irony that someone called Lazarus is suggested as a witness from the dead isn't lost on us: John tells us that when this actually happened it didn't trigger repentance, but a plot to kill Jesus.[2] Verse 31 reads like a passion prediction. Jesus fears the Pharisees will refuse the challenge to change.

The poor and disadvantaged are often in Jesus' mind throughout these chapters of Luke. To whom might God be sending you – and how?

---

[1] Kenneth E Bailey, *Jesus Through Middle Eastern Eyes*, SPCK, 2008, p385 [2] John 11:38–53

BIBLE IN A YEAR: **Genesis 18,19; Matthew 7**

Luke 17:1–10

Watch Yourselves

Read 1 Corinthians 10:12,13 as a way of watching yourself. Invite the Spirit to show you where change or a way out is needed.

Since Jesus turned to address the crowds travelling with him,[1] there's been no mention of the journey continuing. Instead, we read of different groups crowding around Jesus and being addressed in different ways. For example, Luke 16 switches from addressing the disciples to the Pharisees, presumably in the same conversation. Before the journey to Jerusalem resumes (v 11), Jesus challenges the disciples to go further than the Pharisees in three ways.

The first challenge is to live grace. The Pharisees weighed down people with heavy burdens,[2] making it likely that they would stumble, but the disciples are called to do all they can not to do so (vs 1–3). Even more than this, they're to practise forgiveness towards one another, regardless of how often that's required (v 4), seeking a right attentiveness before God as a safeguard (v 3).[3]

The second challenge is to live faithfully. Now identified as apostles, which means those sent by the King with the message of the kingdom, they ask Jesus to increase their faith. Even a tiny amount is enough to do his bidding. The point is not to ask for more, Jesus responds, but to put what faith you do have to work and see it reshape the world around you. Then it grows of its own accord.

The third challenge is to live humbly. The parable of the servant and the master (vs 7–10) reminds us that, however beloved we are by God, he remains our Master. It's not right for us to expect Almighty God to do our bidding. With delight, we get to play our part working with God for the kingdom, but we're challenged to remember that this is an undeserved privilege.

How are you putting your faith to work in the world around you? Ask God for fresh empowerment in doing so and for inspiration for new faithful risks to take.

[1] Luke 14:25 [2] Cf Matt 23:3,4 [3] 1 Cor 4:4

BIBLE IN A YEAR: **Genesis 20,21; Matthew 8**

Kingdom Gratitude

Ingratitude can corrode us from within. Ask God to show if you're focusing too much on what he has not yet done rather than on what he has already done.

The journey to Jerusalem, begun in Luke 9:51, resumes along the border with Samaria. Jesus has sent the seventy-two out ahead of him.[1] Not only are many travelling with him, but Jesus is now expected wherever he goes. A group of people with leprosy, banded together across racial tensions by their desperate plight, seize their opportunity. Standing at a distance – both because they fear making others unclean and because they fear being driven away because their condition provoked loathing – they shout out together as loudly as they can. They want to stop Jesus before he enters the village, from which they were barred. They name Jesus as their Master and implore him to share God's mercy with them.

Halted by their shouts, conscious that they're grasping for the presence of the kingdom, Jesus tells them to go and present themselves to the priests according to the Law. Such an examination was key: being certified as clean by a priest released them from isolation and restored them to community. Then, as they exercise faith in Jesus and obey his instruction, something amazing happens: they are cleansed. In going in faith to obey the Law, they receive the kingdom instead. They are all cleansed, but only one gives proper acknowledgement to Jesus. Feeling it seemingly in his body, he returns full of loud and ecstatic praise. His reverent response is close to worship, but Jesus doesn't refuse it. He simply wonders aloud how the other nine have not been similarly moved. This foreigner, responding in joy, not just from obligation, has discerned the right response. Jesus sends him back to life and community as another whose faith in Jesus, who alone has the authority to heal, has made well.

Ask God to give you the hunger for God's kingdom and a boldness in prayer, returning to your prayer agenda from New Year's Day.

---

[1] See Luke 10:1

BIBLE IN A YEAR: **Genesis 22,23; Psalms 5,6**

Luke 17:20-37

Already and Not Yet

'Jesus Christ is the same yesterday and today and for ever.'[1] Reflect on Jesus' Lordship over your past and your future. Commit to being fruitful in the present.

Speculation is growing. On the way to Jerusalem, both the disciples and the Pharisees want to know what this all means for the kingdom of God.[2] Jesus is challenged about when and where the kingdom will come.

Jesus answers the Pharisees by saying that the kingdom cannot be either diagnosed or located by careful observation. Instead, Jesus insists that the kingdom of God is *already* present in their midst. We have earlier seen Jesus driving out demons 'by the finger of God'.[3] When that happens or people are healed (v 14), the kingdom of God has come. In that sense, the kingdom is *already* present in our midst as the power of the Holy Spirit at work among us.

Jesus then tells the disciples (probably privately), that there's also so much more of the kingdom that is *not yet* present.

There'll be times when they long for its coming (v 22) and people will imagine its presence (v 23), but the disciples are not to be deceived. The *not yet* of the kingdom won't come in a hidden way: when the Son of Man comes,[4] his coming will light up the sky and there will no doubt at all (v 24). Before that can happen, Jesus himself has to choose the kingdom by choosing the cross (v 25).

So the disciples are to live ready. They're to rely on the kingdom present in their midst, even as they wait for it to come in its fullness (facing travails in that waiting). When the day comes, we must not look back, as did Lot's wife, but must run towards Jesus, revealed in his glory, as vultures are drawn from afar to a feast on the ground.

Speculation about the Lord's return isn't fruitful.[5] Instead, ask for more of God's *already* to come in your life and that of your community.

---

[1] Heb 13:8 [2] Cf Luke 19:11 [3] Luke 11:20 [4] See Dan 7:13 [5] Matt 24:36

BIBLE IN A YEAR: **Genesis 24,25; Matthew 9**

An Irrepressible Widow

Pray for Christians in positions of leadership, whether in government, business, public service or the church. Ask God to strengthen them with wisdom and courage.

Luke's introduction suggests that we sometimes lack the stomach for the fight. 'Lose heart' (see v 1, NKJV) is a literal translation where the NIV has 'give up', but the root of this word is cowardice. Jesus is telling us that we sometimes lack the courage to keep praying over the long haul. Jesus wants us to be more like this irrepressible widow. She has no leverage: women had no place in court proceedings at the time. That she has to appear for herself shows that she's isolated with no male relative to take up her cause. Her isolation may well be why she's been exploited. Her lack of means may be why she has lost, through not being able to bribe the judge.

The judge has no interest in justice, people's opinions or God's purposes. He enjoys the position for the power it gives him in the community (and probably the bribes). The widow has no leverage; the judge has no obvious weakness to target. Yet she has the courage to ask and keep on asking. She makes such a persistent nuisance of herself, badgering him shamelessly, that in the end the judge rules justly, simply to shut her up.

Our prayer, Jesus says, is to be as courageous as that, refusing to be denied. What does our prayer say about how we see the God we're approaching in prayer? When we don't persist, we suggest that God is even less interested in doing justice than this pathetic judge. Yet Jesus insists that God's heart is for justice, not delay, and that even shameless badgering won't antagonise him (the last part of verse 7 stresses God's patience towards us). That's the kind of faith the Son of Man longs to see on his return: courageous, persistent faith as shown by this woman.

Faith is opposed to fear as much as doubt. Ask for courage to overcome any fears that make it harder for you to show faith like that of this widow.

BIBLE IN A YEAR: **Genesis 26,27; Matthew 10**

Luke 18:9–17

What Holiness Looks Like

Read 1 John 1:6,7. Ask the Spirit to help you see yourself as you are (with signs where you're growing in holiness, as well as your weaknesses).

Two men go up to the Temple to pray. The context is the 'time of prayer':[1] a time of both corporate worship and private prayer associated with the atonement sacrifices (offered daily at dawn and 3 pm). The sacrifice was offered outside, followed by the reading of a psalm (accompanied by cymbals and trumpets), before the officiating priest went inside to offer incense and attend to the lamps – as Zechariah was doing when he encountered Gabriel:[2] as incense was being burned inside, 'all the assembled worshippers were praying outside'.[3]

Standing apart from others to avoid contact with anyone unclean, the Pharisee is assured of his standing with God and is contemptuous of others (vs 9,11). As intercessory prayer was often said aloud, Jesus may want us to imagine the impact of his words on those close by, such as the tax collector. He's gone further than required in fasting and tithing, he's outdoing others, at least in his own estimation. He asks nothing of God, because he believes nothing is lacking. He's like the ninety-nine who do not realise they need to repent.[4]

In contrast, the tax collector stands at a distance, fearing to come closer. Beating one's breast is unusual[5] and suggests broken-hearted penitence. He dare not look up to heaven. His request is for more than mercy. Remember that this is an atonement sacrifice. His prayer is something like, 'God, make atonement for me, a sinner' (Paul uses a related noun to describe the cross as a 'sacrifice of atonement').[6] He's asking for grace.

Jesus is clear: the tax collector's humble request means that he goes home justified, but the Pharisee's complacent self-praise means that he's disregarded and will be humbled.

Picking up from the beginning of this note, receive God's forgiveness and know his delight in forgiving you. Ask for continued growth in holiness.

---

[1] See Acts 3:1 [2] Luke 1:8–20 [3] Luke 1:10 [4] Luke 15:7 [5] Cf Luke 23:48 [6] Rom 3:25

BIBLE IN A YEAR: **Genesis 28,29; Psalms 7,8**

Psalm 78:40–72

No Enduring City

Paul calls us to remember that 'our citizenship is in heaven'.[1] Reflect on what that means in the light of your relationships, work and church community.

This psalm challenges us to learn from the past and break the repeating cycle in the history of God's people. After an instruction setting out its purpose (vs 1–8), the psalm describes this pattern twice: in verses 9–39 (last Sunday's reading) and in verses 40–72 (today's reading). Both iterations of the pattern describe the Exodus. The first focuses on the parting of the sea and the wilderness (vs 12–16), the second on the plagues and judgement on Egypt (vs 42–55). When it comes to rebellion, the first reflects on the wilderness (vs 17–31), the second addresses their disobedience after settlement in the land (vs 56–64). The first cycle comes to an end with God staying his hand despite knowing their faith isn't wholehearted (vs 32–39).

The second cycle ends on a hopeful note, explaining why the centre of political and religious life has moved to the southern kingdom. God's judgement upon Ephraim (shorthand for the northern kingdom, as its most prominent tribe) has come because of the events of 1 Samuel 4–6 (vs 60–64). God's purpose has still gone forward, however, through a capital being built on the heights of Zion (vs 68,69) and the anointing of a skilful leader with integrity in David, called to shepherd them as a people (vs 70–72).

The psalm was written to warn us to cooperate with God's purpose in the present, by learning from past mistakes. Of course, we know that the settled pattern described in verses 67–72 ends in the Exile, yet even then a root from the tree of Jesse will arise and a king from David's line will establish a kingdom that will never cease.[2] God's purpose – however often diverted – cannot be defeated and will end in a new Jerusalem.[3]

Read Hebrews 13:14. Let's give thanks that the end of our stories will be a new beginning in 'the city that is to come'.

---

[1] Phil 3:20 [2] Isa 11:1,10; 9:7 [3] Rev 21:1-5

BIBLE IN A YEAR: **Genesis 30,31; Matthew 11**

Luke 18:18-30

Wealth and the Kingdom

Read the Ten Commandments in Exodus 20:1–17. Which challenges you the most? How will you respond?

The ruler's question isn't a casual one. Even his unusual address to Jesus as 'Good teacher' (v 18), which Jesus pushes back against to test the man's insight (v 19), suggests that this is a personal question, which matters: what must he do to inherit eternal life? Jesus points him to the commandments. The man replies that he's kept them all since he was a boy, yet clearly this hasn't brought him peace or he wouldn't be asking the question.

Jesus hears the man's sincerity and longing,[1] but he then challenges him about coveting and possessions (the tenth commandment, not previously mentioned). The man has so much, but there is one thing he lacks: his attachment to his possessions makes him unable to choose the kingdom. The irony is that his lack is that he has everything. That is what stops him following Jesus. Literally 'deeply grieved' (v 23) because of his wealth, he cannot follow through. Jesus has compassion for the man's distress and recognises how hard his choice is, but there's no getting away from it: wealth is what stops him receiving the kingdom. For him, it cannot be both/and, it has to be either/or. You can't get a camel through the eye of a needle; this man, though he longs to follow, cannot do so unless he yields up what has such a hold over him.

Wealth as a spiritual problem (not as a sign of blessing) shocks all who are listening (v 26). Peter blurts out that they've done what's required: 'We have left all we had to follow you!' (v 28). Jesus then reassures the disciples that sacrifices made to choose the kingdom of God will not be in vain, but that the challenge to choose the kingdom always comes first.

Ask God to show what stops you seeking his kingdom and righteousness first before all things.[2] Be accountable to another if God shows you need to change.

---

[1] Cf Mark 10:21 [2] Matt 6:33

BIBLE IN A YEAR: **Genesis 32,33; Matthew 12**

More than Coins

Reflect on your sense of God's purpose and calling in your life. Where does it seem clear? Where are you needing greater insight and wisdom?

From the moment he set his face towards Jerusalem,[1] Jesus has been walking towards the cross. He speaks to his disciples on the way about how God's purpose will be fulfilled, but the disciples fail to understand. As they approach Jericho, they're greeted by many who are excited to see Jesus. The buzz of anticipation reaches a blind beggar as the crowds pass by. Intrigued, he asks what's going on. When he hears that it's Jesus, the beggar starts to make a massive racket like the people with leprosy whom Jesus met earlier,[2] desperate not to let the opportunity pass him by. Those leading the way rebuke him, telling him to shut up, but the blind man will not stay in his place. He becomes as outrageously loud as he can manage, shouting, 'Son of David, have mercy on me!' (vs 38,39).

Jesus pauses on the way to the cross, perhaps intrigued by the blind man's insight into his identity as the one who will claim David's kingdom. Far from leaving him, rebuked, in his place, Jesus commands him to be brought near. The beggar had asked for mercy, so Jesus asks him to clarify what he wants (is it more than coins for food?). The man has the faith to proclaim Jesus as Lord and to ask (literally) that he may see again. Echoing the words that he had quoted in Nazareth,[3] Jesus proclaims recovery of sight for the blind. With sight restored, the man chooses the kingdom and follows Jesus, full of ecstatic praise. Even those who'd wanted him to stay in his place join in.

The contrast in today's passage between what Jesus does for others and what will be done to him is stark. Still he walks the way of the cross, still he chooses the kingdom.

Remember those particularly on your heart. Read Isaiah 61:1–3 and pray for Jesus the Anointed One to minister to them in these ways.

---

[1] Luke 9:51 [2] Luke 17:12,13 [3] Luke 4:18

BIBLE IN A YEAR: **Genesis 34–36; Matthew 13**

Luke 19:1–10

Jesus the Protector

Reflect on how you came to faith. How unexpected was that to your friends and family? Pray for those known to you who seem to be impervious to the gospel.

The streets of Jericho are lined with people excited to see Jesus, though they're disappointed that he is just passing through. Anyone too short to see Jesus would have been ushered to the front. But Zacchaeus can't risk that. His job leading the local tax farmers means he's detested locally. Too short to see from the back, he daren't go to the front. He fears the locals will close ranks against him or even assault him. Desperate to see Jesus without being seen, he runs ahead and climbs a tree outside Jericho (things Middle Eastern adults never do).[1]

Sycamore-fig trees offer good cover, but Zacchaeus is still spotted. It's unclear whether Jesus is the first to spot him. Rather, I wonder if, when Jesus reaches the spot in verse 5, the crowd is enjoying abusing their chief tax collector caught humiliatingly in a tree! Their shouted abuse may have revealed Zacchaeus' name to Jesus, rather than the Spirit. The situation is ugly. Zacchaeus is at real risk of assault. Jesus intervenes. Calling Zacchaeus by name, Jesus invites himself to stay at the house of the most despised man in the town (v 5). Everyone is astonished, not least because you never invite yourself anywhere. Inviting yourself to that man's house is unimaginable. Zacchaeus scrambles down hurriedly and welcomes Jesus as a guest (and protector) with joy (v 6).

In placing Zacchaeus under his protection, Jesus makes himself the subject of angry muttering (v 7). How can the Messiah refuse their hospitality, then go to be the guest of such a hated sinner? Zacchaeus understands that Jesus has taken a huge risk on his behalf. At the banquet Zacchaeus throws in Jesus' honour, he responds by promising restitution and justice. As Jesus proclaims, today salvation has come to this house.

This story beloved of Sunday schools has a hard edge to it. Where might God be calling you to show similar courage on other people's behalf?

[1] Kenneth E Bailey, *Jesus Through Middle Eastern Eyes*, SPCK, 2008, p177–179

BIBLE IN A YEAR: **Genesis 37,38; Psalm 9**

Choosing the King

Peter tells us to be 'faithful stewards of God's grace in its various forms'.[1] How are you serving Christ your King with your gifts?

In addressing the question of when the kingdom would come, Jesus compares himself in verse 12 to a candidate for kingship going to the highest authority to ask for the right to rule (as Herod had done in Rome). Those disputing his claim (v 14) are the Pharisees and the ruling elite.

The gifts to the ten servants aren't massive (about four months' wages for a day labourer), but while his claim is being adjudicated, the master is asking for them publicly to trade in his name. Standing up for him when he's been confirmed in office requires no courage, but doing so while waiting for his return is a risky, costly loyalty. If it goes against their master, then everything is over for them as well.

That's why the master rewards the loyalty of the first two servants: 'because you were faithful in a least thing' (v 17, translating literally), take charge of cities.

It's about faithfulness, not profit. The increase of responsibility for them both is huge because they've been trustworthy – but the third servant's speech is outrageous. If he really thought his master was like this, as the master points out, surely he would have put the money to work with the bankers? Instead, he's waited out the interval, not wanting to be publicly loyal until there's no longer any risk in doing so. Even now he's confident he'll suffer no real punishment for his inactivity, a confidence in his master that turns out to be justified for he's only deprived of the money entrusted to him. He's risked nothing and suffered no loss.

As with other parables, this one is also left unfinished. The judgement on the king's opponents is announced but not actually performed. Everyone, disciples and opponents, is challenged to consider how they will wait for the King's return.

While waiting for the King's return in glory, we're challenged to show costly loyalty. What might choosing the King look like for you?

---

[1] 1 Pet 4:10

BIBLE IN A YEAR: **Genesis 39,40; Matthew 14**

Leviticus 1–15

GOD IN THE CENTRE

As Dr Felix Chingota from Malawi explained, the book of Leviticus is at the centre of the Pentateuch, not only structurally but also theologically.[1] In Genesis, our first parents sinned and were expelled from God's presence in the Garden of Eden. God initiated the process of their restoration and chose Abraham and his race as the means of fostering grace in the sin-polluted world.[2] In Exodus, God liberated the people of Israel from slavery and made a covenant with them. They soon broke faith with him, but in response to Moses' intercession,[3] God instructed him to build the Tabernacle as the focus of his presence. It is in the book of Leviticus that this was actually realised. What Numbers and Deuteronomy do is to continue the story of the ups and downs of Israel's journey to the Promised Land in this new dispensation under the leadership of Moses.

Named after the tribe of Levi, central to worship in the Tabernacle, Leviticus describes in meticulous detail the laws, the rituals and the rules that govern everyday conduct. What is the point, we may well ask, of anointing ears and thumbs and big toes with blood, splattering blood on the altar and sprinkling it seven times, as we see in the book? Experiences with my grandfather, an African traditional medicine man (*Babaláwo*, literally 'Father of Mysteries'), gave me an appreciation of the awe, the solemnity and the faithful devotion – and also the lessons in obedience – which go with seemingly pointless rituals common to primitive religion. Unique to this particular narrative, however, is that it is all directed to the worship of a holy God who makes it clear that his people should be holy too. Not surprisingly, we find sprinkled through these chapters the constant refrain: 'Be holy, for I am holy.'

Emmanuel Oladipo

---

[1] Felix Chingota, in *Africa Bible Commentary*, ed Tokunboh Adeyemo, Word Alive Publishers, 2006, p129–130 [2] See Gen 12:2,3 [3] Exod 33:12–17

Burned up for God

'Take my life and let it be / consecrated, Lord, to thee / ... Take myself, and I will be / ever, only, all for thee.'[1]

The reason why people were to bring burnt offerings to the priest is specified: 'to make atonement for you' (v 4). It could be a bull from the herd of the well-to-do, a lamb or a goat from the flock of the averagely endowed, or a dove or pigeon which even the poorest could afford. Thus atonement was available and accessible to all, irrespective of social position or possessions.

The burnt offering is the first of five sacrifices described in Leviticus. There are four facts worth noting about the rituals involved. First, there is the laying-on of hands (v 4). This practice conferred spiritual responsibility and/or blessing on the person involved.[2] Here in Leviticus, responsibility for sin is placed on the sacrificial animals, perhaps anticipating how it was finally to be placed on the crucified Saviour on our behalf. Second, and rather strangely, the internal organs and the legs are to be washed clean before being burned (v 9). This, together with the fact that only spotless animals could be brought for sacrifice, highlights the fact that our holy God demands purity from his people. Third, blood had a special place in the ritual (vs 5,11,15), for 'the life of the flesh is in the blood'.[3] Finally, although the priests, and sometimes the people who brought the offerings, can eat of other sacrifices,[4] this one is dedicated to God in its entirety and so it is completely consumed by fire.

In Yoruba traditional African religion, there is a saying that 'When you've led a goat to the shrine you let go of the leash'. When we offer ourselves to God as a living sacrifice, how complete is the offering? Do we hold on to the leash in some parts of our lives?

'The problem with living sacrifices is that they try to crawl off the altar.'[5] How does this apply to you in the light of Romans 12:1?

---

[1] Frances Ridley Havergal, 1836–79 [2] Eg Num 8:10,11; Luke 4:40; Acts 13:3 [3] Lev 17:11, AV [4] Lev 5:13; Deut 15:19,20 [5] Anon

BIBLE IN A YEAR: **Genesis 41,42; Matthew 15**

Peace, Feasts, Fellowship

Praise God today for enabling you to accept his invitation to the wedding feast of the Lamb.[1]

In chapter 2, we read about the grain offering, which is the second of five offerings described in Leviticus. This chapter tells us about the third, the fellowship or peace offering. Further details are to be found in 7:11–21. It differs from other sacrifices in two respects. First, it is not commanded by God but may be offered as a voluntary act of thanksgiving and worship. Second, it is the one sacrifice from which not only the priest may eat but the person making the offering and their family and friends as well.

Based on the meaning of the Hebrew root word which is linked to 'shalom', Bible translations refer to it both as the peace offering and the fellowship offering. Peace is an essential prerequisite of fellowship, since no two people can be in fellowship if they are not at peace with each other.

Anyone making this offering was seeking to experience joyful fellowship with God in spite of all their human flaws. It foreshadows that peace we have through Jesus Christ, which makes possible our fellowship with our holy Creator God. The result is peace in our own heart, leading to peace with others as we keep growing in the grace of God.

In the last supper Jesus Christ had with his disciples, he shared with them the bread and the wine, representing his body and his blood. He instituted it as a memorial in which he invites us to share a fellowship meal with him in the here and now, along with our fellow believers. He has sent out a blanket invitation to all the world, which anyone and everyone is free to accept. The day is coming when we shall be privileged to share a banquet with him – the wedding feast of the Lamb!

'Take and eat this in remembrance that Christ died for thee, and feed on him in thy heart by faith, with thanksgiving.'[2] Do you?

---

[1] Rev 19:9 [2] Words at giving of Communion in the Anglican Church, *Book of Common Prayer*

BIBLE IN A YEAR: **Genesis 43,44; Psalm 10**

Psalm 79

The Suffering Church

'They called out in a loud voice, "How long, Sovereign Lord, holy and true, until you judge the inhabitants of the earth and avenge our blood?"'[1]

I have a good idea of how Asaph was feeling when he wrote this psalm. Fellow Christians in my country of Nigeria do. We know what it is to have our land ravaged by the enemy, to have our places of worship desecrated and burnt down and to have our leaders murdered along with many of their flock (vs 1–3). In all this, we are not alone. Verse 5 is a plaintive cry we share with the suffering church in many countries of the world today.

Asaph saw his circumstances as a consequence of the sins of past generations (v 8). As Christians today, we do not have that luxury. We have to accept full responsibility for our own failings. Taking note of God's promise to King Solomon at the dedication of the Temple, we must humble ourselves before the Lord and seek his face in earnest prayer so that he will hear from heaven, forgive our sins and heal our land.[2] Sadly, however, we often fail to turn from our wicked ways!

We share in the desperation of this psalmist and his desire that God's name be glorified (vs 8,9). We know God to be our Saviour in a more comprehensive way than he could have imagined (v 9). We live in the age of grace, and so we know better now than to call down God's wrath on our enemies (vs 6,12). The desire of our hearts is, as Paul enjoined Timothy: 'that God will grant them repentance leading them to a knowledge of the truth, and that they will come to their senses and escape from the trap of the devil'.[3] This is what turns Saul of Tarsus into Paul the apostle; and it is our prayer for those who persecute God's people everywhere.

Find out details of one country where the church is being persecuted and make a regular habit of praying for them.

[1] Rev 6:10 [2] 2 Chr 7:14 [3] 2 Tim 2:25,26

BIBLE IN A YEAR: **Genesis 45,46; Matthew 16**

Leviticus 4:1 – 5:13

'Mea Culpa!'

Can you think of some unintentional sin you committed recently? What did you do about it?

The late Rabbi Jonathan Sacks described in a short video three types of unintentional sin covered by the sin offering in Judaism.[1] One is to do something without knowing that it was sin. Another is to know, but to do it in an act of carelessness, such as breaking the Sabbath because you thought it was Friday. The third is to know it to be sin but to do it unknowingly – breaking the speed limit, for instance, because you relied on a faulty speedometer. There is nothing anyone can do to erase such human errors, but God provided the way to make it right with him. Here we have full descriptions for the process of atonement – for priests (4:3–12), for secular leaders (vs 22–26), for ordinary individuals (vs 27–31) and for the community at large (vs 13–21).

From our human point of view, unintentional sin is really no big deal. As CS Lewis put it, 'I am not angry with a man who trips me up by accident; I am angry with a man who tries to trip me up, even if he does not succeed. Yet the first has hurt me and the second has not'.[2] Surely, it would be charitable of God to ignore unintentional sin and concentrate his ire on wilful violation of his Law? Whether intended or not, however, sin separates us from God and always leaves its poisonous stain behind. We may not always see that stain, but God does. Regardless of how it comes about, God takes all sin very seriously.

In that video, Jonathan Sacks explained that animal sacrifices removed the stain of sin. For us, they are merely a pointer to what was to come. It is the blood of Jesus Christ which deals with the root of sin, not merely its stain.[3]

Think about how much David's prayer in Psalm 51 applies to you today.

---

[1] Jonathan Sacks, https://youtu.be/YSjFs6fa2WQ [2] CS Lewis, *Mere Christianity*, Macmillan, 1943, p28
[3] 1 John 1:7–10

BIBLE IN A YEAR: **Genesis 47,48; Matthew 17**

Guilt and Restitution

'And forgive us our debts, as we also have forgiven our debtors.'[1]

The last one of these sacrifices in Leviticus, the guilt offering, is sometimes termed 'the trespass offering' or 'the reparation offering'. This is because it covers sins which involve a breach of faith regarding any of the Lord's holy things (5:15). Evidently, this sort of sin calls for restitution; and the penalty rate is set at 20 per cent of the value of the object concerned (v 16). Someone who violates a neighbour's trust is put in the same category (6:1–7). This is especially relevant when they take the Lord's name in vain by lying on oath about their wrongdoing.

We see here that God also accepts something other than animal sacrifices. Our reading includes the grain offering (6:14–23) which, like the burnt offering, is a voluntary act of worship. The first person on record to make such an offering was Cain.[2] Unfortunately, his offering was not acceptable to God. Here we have the proof that the reason was not because, unlike his brother Abel, he had brought a vegetable rather than an animal sacrifice involving the shedding of blood. As the prophets reminded Israel time and again, it is the disposition of the human heart which determines whether or not an offering is acceptable to God.[3]

For us today, Zacchaeus is an excellent example of making restitution.[4] He acknowledged his sin, accepted the salvation which Jesus Christ offered him and, of his own volition, decided to right the many wrongs of his life and profession by making costly reparations. Whereas the sacrifices in Leviticus are described as 'an aroma pleasing to the LORD' (6:15,21), it is people such as you and I who are described in such terms in the New Testament.[5]

Have you ever had a significant experience of making restitution? Can you think of anything calling for one at the moment? Make this an item of praise or prayer.

[1] Matt 6:12 [2] Gen 4:2–5 [3] Eg Jer 6:19,20 [4] Luke 19:1–10 [5] 2 Cor 2:14–16

BIBLE IN A YEAR: **Genesis 49,50; Matthew 18**

Leviticus 6:24 – 7:38

God is not a Bad Employer

Praise God and pray to him for the personal welfare, both physical and spiritual, of your spiritual leaders.

Our God is supremely generous. The bountiful manner in which he provides for his servants is a fitting demonstration of this fact. The Levites were not apportioned an inheritance among the tribes of Israel.[1] However, the Law made special provision to cater for their welfare. As we have already seen from our readings, it was a very generous portion of meat, grain, oil and bread from each sacrifice, whether individual or communal.

This provision for the priests and the Levites was intrinsically linked to the obedience and generosity of God's people. So long as they kept bringing their mandatory sacrifices as well as their voluntary offerings, there would be more than enough for those whose job it was to nurture their spiritual welfare. If the people failed to do their part, then the priests would lose their only means of sustenance and would have to look elsewhere for their livelihood. Thus, they would abandon their duty of spiritual care for the people and God's blessing would be withdrawn from them. Sadly, to their great cost, this was a repeated occurrence in the history of Israel.[2] The priests and the Levites, too, had to be faithful to their calling. They could not afford to take for granted either God's abundant provision for them or the people's generosity. That would also incur God's displeasure, as was the case with Hophni and Phinehas, sons of Eli the priest.[3]

The principles remain the same with us. God expects us to make adequate provision for those he has chosen to be our spiritual leaders in the church at every level, unless, like Paul, they are able and willing to provide for themselves.[4] However, Christian leaders who enrich themselves at the expense of God's people will have to answer to him!

Read 1 Corinthians 4:2 and pray for the Lord to make you faithful in his service, whatever may be your calling.

---

[1] Deut 18:2 [2] Eg 2 Chr 11:14; Neh 13:10 [3] 1 Sam 2:22–36 [4] 1 Cor 9:13–18

BIBLE IN A YEAR: Exodus 1,2; Psalms 11,12

Consecration for Service

'He has covered me with the robe of righteousness'.[1] Thank God for this experience in your life.

The first seven chapters of Leviticus describe the different sacrifices and how they were offered. This chapter tells us of the consecration of priests responsible for presenting them to God. Moses took due care to do what God ordained and in the manner God prescribed. It was all full of symbols with deep and far-reaching spiritual significance.

Aaron and his sons were brought before God and the entire assembly of the people of Israel. Before anything else, they were washed with water (v 6). Jesus Christ was later to make the point that such a washing was an indication of the full cleansing which enables sinful people to become acceptable to our impeccably holy God.[2] After this, they had their everyday clothes replaced with ornate priestly ceremonial garments (vs 7–9,13). Zechariah's vision helps us to understand the import of this symbol in the spiritual realm.[3] Even more significant are Paul's words that when we are washed with the water of baptism, we are clothed 'with Christ'![4]

Then, there were the sacrifices, starting with the bull on whose head Aaron and his sons laid their hands before it was slaughtered (vs 14–16). The blood and different parts of the carcass were variously treated 'as the LORD commanded Moses' (v 17). Then came the ram, which was consumed entirely by fire as a whole burnt offering devoted to the Lord. Together, they all point to Jesus Christ the Lamb of God, who was sacrificed to atone for our sin. Finally, there was the anointing with oil for consecration, a solemn dedication for sacred purpose and service. Today we have a much more sacred anointing. It is not made of vegetable oil and dispensed with the hands of a priest. Our anointing is God's Holy Spirit conferred on us by God himself.[5]

What light does Hebrews 9 throw on this passage for us?

[1] Isa 61:10, NKJV [2] John 13:10 [3] Zech 3:1–5 [4] Gal 3:27 [5] 2 Cor 1:21,22

BIBLE IN A YEAR: **Exodus 3,4; Matthew 19**

A Royal Priesthood

Praise the Lord today for your priestly calling in Christ and pray to be faithful to the end.

With the consecration of Aaron and his sons, Moses now had a team to share with him the burden of the spiritual leadership of the nation. Notice what Aaron was told to do in verse 7. This was the first of many occasions in the course of his ministry when he would make atonement first for himself and then for the people. It starts with the sin offering to obtain cleansing and forgiveness before approaching God's holy presence. Then, there is the whole burnt offering to signify total dedication to God and to him alone. The peace offering followed, being the rite signifying their fellowship and communion with God. They got it all right; and God put his unmistakeable stamp of approval on the blessing pronounced on his people (vs 23,24).

God calls different people for different tasks in his vineyard; and the equipping required for each calling is different. Moses, for example, was never required to follow any of these procedures to gain access to God and to minister to his people. His call pre-dated the Law and his role was unique. However, he too had to take God's holiness seriously and obey his Word to the letter. Just one momentary lapse of judgement was to cost him dearly![1]

We too are called to be priests of the most high and holy God.[2] Our own calling is in a new dispensation which post-dates the Law, since all the demands of the Law have been fulfilled on our behalf by Jesus Christ.[3] This qualifies us to enter into the holy presence of God and commune with him as with a friend and to announce the good news of his peace to a troubled world. What a calling!

Christ calls us too to be his priests.[4] What does this mean for you in practice?

[1] Num 20:7-13 [2] 1 Pet 2:4,5 [3] Rom 8:3,4 [4] 1 Pet 2:9

BIBLE IN A YEAR: **Exodus 5,6; Matthew 20**

God is a Consuming Fire

Pray that you will always act with due reverence as you exercise your freedom to approach God freely.

One thing Nadab and Abihu could not plead is ignorance. By word and example, again and again, Moses had made it all too clear what God required of them as priests. Whatever got into them to lead them into such flagrant disobedience? Verse 9 makes us wonder – was it perhaps wine?

Based on passages such as this, some people make a false distinction between the God of the Old Testament and the God of the New. They see an angry and vindictive God in the Old Testament but a loving and compassionate God in the New. The truth, however, is that God is the same yesterday, today and for ever. The only difference is that, incrementally through the Bible, he gives us an ever-growing understanding of his ways in the process of progressive revelation. God did not take a light view of sin in the New Testament any more than he did in the Old. The fate of Nadab and Abihu here is no different from what befell Ananias and his wife Sapphira in the New Testament.[1] Nor was he any less compassionate in the Old Testament than in the New, as demonstrated in his gracious dealing with Nineveh.[2]

Thankfully, the sort of instant judgement which Nadab and Abihu, and Ananias and Sapphira, experienced is not currently the norm. People do not fall down dead on account of their flippancy at the communion table. The God who is not willing that anyone should perish gives us more of an opportunity to repent.[3] Surely, this is no licence for taking for granted the holiness of God! We do not want to learn the hard way that now, as always, our 'God is a consuming fire'.[4]

'It is a dreadful thing to fall into the hands of the living God.'[5] How can this be a real danger for us and for our church today?

---

[1] Acts 5:1-11 [2] Jonah 3:10; 4:10,11 [3] Ps 130:3; 2 Pet 3:9 [4] Heb 12:29 [5] Heb 10:31

BIBLE IN A YEAR: **Exodus 7,8; Psalms 13,14**

Psalm 80

Israel's Failure and Ours

'If you, LORD, kept a record of sins, Lord, who could stand?'[1]

The very fact that God is the Shepherd of Israel is enough to guarantee her security (v 1). This is the Good Shepherd of whom David speaks in Psalm 23. Under his loving care, everything the people required to be a prosperous nation at peace with itself and with their neighbours was richly provided for them. That was the previous enviable state for which the psalmist now pines (vs 3,7,14). The mention of Ephraim and Manasseh in verse 2 would seem to indicate that it is the northern kingdom that is in question here, perhaps when it was under the yoke of the Assyrians.

How did it come to this? Sadly, Israel demonstrated time and again that it had failed to learn its lesson from the fate of Nadab and Abihu on the consequences of disobedience. This was especially true of the northern kingdom under its unbroken succession of godless kings. The people rebelled against the God of their salvation and he abandoned them just as they had been warned in the Law given to them by Moses. Therefore they were destroyed by other nations, for whom they were meant to model God's grace and favour in a lost world (vs 12,13).[2]

We too must take the same lesson to heart. In the Lord Jesus Christ we have blessings which are the envy of the watching world.[3] Our conduct, however, is not always in keeping with what we know and proclaim. Mahatma Gandhi of India once explained to the Christian missionary, Dr E Stanley Jones: 'Oh, I don't reject your Christ. I love your Christ. It is just that so many of you Christians are so unlike your Christ.'[4] How sad!

Paul enjoined other believers to imitate him, just as he imitated Christ.[5] Pray from now on to be able to say the same.

---

[1] Ps 130:3 [2] Compare Gen 22:18 [3] Matt 5:16 [4] Jude Thaddeus Langeh Basebang, 'Gandhi's message to Christians' in *Africa needs Gandhi!*, Prabhat Prakashan, 2020 [5] 1 Cor 11:1

BIBLE IN A YEAR: **Exodus 9,10; Matthew 21**

Strange Food Laws

Thank God for giving you all the food you need and more. Pray for wisdom to eat in a responsible manner, always mindful of the needs of others.

We can only speculate as to the reasoning behind the classification of what may or may not be consumed as food according to these laws. Meat from animals which have cloven hoofs and chew the cud does not taste any better or provide more healthy sustenance than those which are banned for eating! The same is true of sea creatures with scales and fins and the birds and insects specified in our reading. What, then, was the purpose of these laws and of what relevance are they for us today?

God wants us to eat and to eat well. That is the way he has designed our bodies. However, right from the beginning, God saw it fit to introduce some discipline regarding what we eat.[1] Sometimes, the reason for the prohibition is explained, as for the sanctity of blood, but in other instances the reason remains a mystery. However, one thing is clear. In giving his laws for Israel to obey, Israel's God was making a distinction between them and all the other nations on earth.[2] Regardless of whether the people of Israel understood the underlying reasons, every one of God's laws was for their good.[3]

Today we are at liberty to eat anything and everything we fancy, since Jesus Christ has delivered us from the demands of the Law. Being a vegetarian or a non-vegetarian does nothing to improve our spiritual standing with God. It is still important, all the same, to exercise strict discipline in what we eat or do not eat. We have a responsibility to take good care of our body, which is the temple of the Holy Spirit. Also, even when what we choose to eat may do us no harm, we should be careful to consider its impact on the spiritual and physical well-being of others.[4]

Ask God to keep you mindful of the welfare of others in every area of your life.

---

[1] Gen 2:17; 9:4 [2] Deut 4:8 [3] Deut 10:12,13 [4] Rom 14:20,21; 1 Cor 8:8–13

BIBLE IN A YEAR: **Exodus 11,12; Matthew 22**

Leviticus 12

The Virtues in the Blood

Are there rituals to do with blood in your culture or other cultures known to you? Pray about them and the people involved today.

Israel had just come out of its bondage from Egypt, redeemed by the Lord who had chosen the people be his own.[1] This was the background to the Law that he gave to the people on Mount Sinai. Obeying it is part of the process of making Israel the holy nation God wants it to be, an example to the rest of the world.

Our passage today has to do with the purification of women from the blood of childbirth. Different cultures have their own rituals connected with the three main stages of life: birth, marriage and death; this is part of what God ordained for his people. Why does the blood of childbirth make a woman unclean? Does it perhaps relate to the curse of Eden, regarding the pain of childbirth?[2] No one knows for sure, but this ritual uncleanness is evidently linked to that which attends the discharge of bodily fluids (v 2; and see chapter 15, which also addresses male discharges). Both here (vs 2,5) and elsewhere in the Law,[3] there is a clear distinction in practice based on the gender of the child.

Whatever the case, this ritual purification involves the shedding of animal blood: a burnt offering in thanksgiving, followed by a second sacrifice as a sin offering. A lamb is the preferred animal; and we can readily see how this looks forward to the one whom John the Baptist addressed as 'the Lamb of God, who takes away the sin of the world!'[4] Significantly, the parents of Jesus fell into the class of those too poor to afford a lamb for this sacrifice when the Son of God came into our world (v 8).[5]

There are about 100,000 miles of blood vessels in the human body. Find out more about the blood and praise the Lord in the words of Psalm 139:14.

[1] Exod 19:5,6 [2] Gen 3:16 [3] Lev 27:2-6 [4] John 1:29 [5] Luke 2:22-24

BIBLE IN A YEAR: Exodus 13,14; Matthew 23

Medicine Then and Now

'Praise the Lord ... who forgives all your sins and heals all your diseases.'[1]

God speaks to his people in any number of ways, both in Bible times and today. He spoke to Moses, at different times, through an audible voice at the burning bush, through the wise counsel of his father-in-law and face to face.[2] In dealing with medical issues here, could he, perhaps, have spoken through people who had trained and served in Egypt? If so, God's Holy Spirit filtered out every idea and practice that would do more harm than good, including the use of noxious, revolting ingredients such as animal faeces and human urine by the famed physicians of ancient Egypt!

Significantly, many concepts here remain relevant to the practice of medicine to this day: the place of careful observation in the process of diagnosis (vs 3,20,25, etc), the need for isolation to prevent the spread of diseases, especially when their nature remains unknown (vs 4,5), the incineration of contaminated objects that cannot be safely restored (vs 52,55,57), meticulous cleanliness (vs 34,58) and the active cooperation of the patient in the entire process.

In African traditional religion, as in ancient civilisations ranging from Egypt to China and the Incas of Peru, the medical function was intricately linked to priestcraft; and it was the same in Israel. My grandfather, as an African healer, not only concocted herbs and potions but used incantations to invoke the power of his pagan gods on his drugs; and he offered sacrifices aimed at combating the spiritual roots of ailments. What a privilege we have as Christians! We are able to invoke the power of the Almighty Creator God through our prayers as we apply modern medicine to combat both the symptoms and the root cause of disease.

Praise God for progress in medical and other research that improves the lot of humankind and for our progressive understanding of his Word and world.

[1] Ps 103:2,3 [2] Exod 3:1-4; 18:17-26; 33:11

BIBLE IN A YEAR: **Exodus 15,16; Psalms 15,16**

Leviticus 14

Am I my Brother's Keeper?

Thank God that he cares for your welfare today, even though you do not always understand his ways.

Cleanliness, they say, is next to godliness. Many Jews, however, took it even further at the time of Jesus Christ. To them, cleanliness, in the ritual sense, amounted to godliness. They were horrified, for example, that his disciples ate without giving their hands the full, approved, ceremonial cleansing, because 'The Pharisees and all the Jews do not eat unless they give their hands a ceremonial washing'.[1] Jesus explained why they were wrong; but he had no problem with the sort of washing in our reading today. Indeed, when he healed the people affected with the dreaded disease termed 'leprosy' in those days, he actually sent them to the priests as this Law prescribed.[2]

In dealing with the Covid-19 pandemic and similar afflictions of the modern era, we still follow very closely a lot of what this ancient text prescribed. As we saw in chapter 13, all infectious skin diseases were immediately isolated for a period of two weeks.[3] At the end, the priest carried out tests to determine whether or not the patient presented a danger to others.[4] When he was satisfied that the infection had cleared, he confirmed it with prescribed sacrifices; and the washing of persons and objects were part of the prescription (vs 8,9,47).

There is much that we do not understand about the accompanying rituals, steeped as they are in symbolism. The reasons why clean birds are slaughtered in a clay pot over running water, the anointing on the right earlobe, the thumb of the right hand and the big toe of the right foot, are not revealed to us. All in all, the emphasis on preventing the spread of the disease was key. Here, as elsewhere throughout Scripture, we are called to mind the well-being of others.[5]

Cain asked, 'Am I my brother's keeper?'[6] In what way is this part of your Christian witness?

---

[1].Mark 7:1–8 [2] Matt 8:4 [3] Lev 13:4,5 [4] Lev 13;27,28 [5] Phil 2:4 [6] Gen 4:9

BIBLE IN A YEAR: **Exodus 17,18; Matthew 24**

Clean Body and Soul

'An ounce of prevention is worth a pound of cure.'[1] Pray for wisdom to take all necessary steps to keep yourself in good physical and spiritual health.

We cannot equate ancient medicine with ours today, and God's dealings with Israel reflect the times. This chapter contains instructions for dealing with the discharge of bodily fluids, both the natural and the unusual, in both men and women. In a world without antibiotics, there was very little that medical science had to offer to patients should such fluids be infected. Notice how often the word 'wash' occurs in the text. The main strategy was to take hygienic precautions by keeping body, utensils and clothing as clean as was possible under the prevailing conditions, and to avoid all physical contacts.

This was the world of the woman who had a flow of blood for 12 years before she was healed by Jesus. She had suffered many things from physicians and had spent all she had to no avail.[2] We are not told that the woman's illness had anything to do with personal sin. There is a link, however, between all illnesses and the fallen nature of our world – a good reason for the sin offering required in this and other similar laws (vs 15,30,31). Evidently, God links all of this with his holiness and the standard of purity he expects from those who belong to him.

The people of Israel were to separate themselves 'from things that make them unclean' (v 31). The same is true of us as the community of God's people and also as individual followers of the Lord Jesus Christ. According to the writer of Jude, it involves 'hating even the clothing stained by corrupted flesh'.[3]

'Come out from them and be separate'.[4] In what ways are these words relevant to us today?

[1] Benjamin Franklin, 1706–90 [2] Mark 5:25–34 [3] Jude 23 [4] 2 Cor 6:17

BIBLE IN A YEAR: Exodus 19,20; Matthew 25

Scripture Union

By purchasing *Encounter with God*, you are helping to support Scripture Union's mission with children and young people. Thank you!

Subscribe to our free supporter and prayer magazine at **su.org.uk/ connectingyou**

REJOICE ALWAYS!

Luke tells how Paul and his companions came to Thessalonica, a town on the northern coast of the Aegean Sea, near Philippi. In response to his preaching in the synagogue over a few weeks, 'some of the Jews' joined them, 'as did a large number of God-fearing Greeks and not a few prominent women'.[1] This was the start of the young church to which Paul wrote 1 Thessalonians, probably a few months after he had left them and arrived in Corinth, around AD 50. This letter was followed at some later date by 2 Thessalonians. Paul's reference to how the Thessalonians 'turned to God from idols' suggests that the church was probably dominated by the Gentile converts.[2]

Luke describes how 'other Jews' in Thessalonica reacted with violence.[3] The Thessalonians' experience of significant persecution is a recurring theme in both letters: much of Paul's theology seems to develop from this. Their Christ-like endurance and joy in the midst of suffering are evidence of their calling and demonstrations of God's work in them. Christ's longed-for salvation, and his judgement, are dominant themes, but their hope in the Lord is not for the future only: Paul writes of how the Holy Spirit empowers and sanctifies their present life, individually and communally.

2 Thessalonians contains a cryptic section concerning the 'man of lawlessness', which can put readers off.[4] However, the letter is interesting for its hidden christology: a benediction puts 'our Lord Jesus Christ' in front of God our Father;[5] and the overthrowing of the lawless one is done by Jesus, in place of God, in an allusion to Isaiah.[6] Above all, these letters, 1 Thessalonians in particular, overflow with a sense of joy. Paul is delighted by the faith, love and hope of the new converts.

Amy Hole

FOR FURTHER READING

Victor Paul Furnish, *1 Thessalonians, 2 Thessalonians*, Abingdon Press, 2007
Gene L Green, *The Letters to the Thessalonians*, Apollos, 2002
Ben Witherington III, *1 and 2 Thessalonians: A Socio-Rhetorical Commentary*, Eerdmans, 2006

[1] See Acts 17:1–4, TNIV [2] 1 Thess 1:9 [3] Acts 17:5–9 [4] 2 Thess 2 [5] 2 Thess 2:16 [6] 2 Thess 2:8; Isa 11:4

1 Thessalonians 1

Joy to the World

'O Lord, open our lips / and our mouth shall proclaim your praise.'[1]

Recently, I stayed on holiday near a friary. Early each morning the bells would ring out, calling the monks to prayer and advertising to the whole neighbourhood that Christ was being worshipped. Paul adopts a similar image to tell the Thessalonians how the Lord's message 'rang out' from them across the whole region (v 8); the Greek verb more precisely means to 'resound' or 'roar like thunder'.[2] Their example communicated the gospel so effectively that Paul didn't need to tell other people about their faith – other people told him about it! This seems extraordinary in a pre-internet, pre-printing-press world. How did the Thessalonians witness to so many outside their immediate area? Well, Paul says that they became a 'model' (v 7) for other believers because they had received the gospel with the joy of the Holy Spirit, despite this involving 'severe suffering',

presumably from persecution (v 6). In so doing, they imitated not only the apostles but also Jesus himself, who endured the cross for 'the joy that was set before him'.[3] This is the kind of example that really talks. The reason they could act like this was because they had received the gospel powerfully through the Holy Spirit and were fully convinced of it: it was never just 'words' for them (v 5).

The church is called to communicate the good news of Jesus Christ to all people, everywhere. Alongside preaching and programmes, do we need to reconnect with the incredible truth that God loves us, and rediscover by God's grace the utter joy of the Holy Spirit, whatever our outward circumstances? Let us pray that, as God's Spirit lives in us together, our faith will roar across the world, just as the faith of the Thessalonians did years ago.

Unusually, Paul describes the whole church, not one individual, as a 'model' to others. Be encouraged, and encourage others, that we're never alone: our witness is a joint effort.

---

[1] From Morning Prayer, *Common Worship*, Church House Publishing, 2000, p30 [2] Witherington, *1 and 2 Thessalonians*, Eerdmans, 2006, p73 [3] Heb 12:2

BIBLE IN A YEAR: **Exodus 21,22; Psalm 17**

Psalm 81

Saved but Stubborn

'O Love that wilt not let me go, / I rest my weary soul in thee.'[1]

This is a psalm in two parts. It starts on a note of exuberant worship, with a call to celebrate a corporate festival marking God's action in freeing the Israelites from slavery in Egypt. Then, from verse 6 onwards, our attention shifts. It's as though we have been raised up, out of the throng of noisy praise, to a place where we can hear the very voice of God.

God's words are extremely revealing. The difficulty he pinpoints is that the Israelites do not seem to understand, or even want to know, what they were saved for. Having been rescued from captivity in Egypt, they are refusing to listen to God (v 11). It's as though they think they no longer have any need for him, now that he has 'removed the burden from their shoulders' (v 6); 'would not submit to', in verse 11, may be more accurately rendered 'did not want'.[2] God, however, longs for them to know the full nature of their salvation: to live with him as his people, to listen to him and to follow his ways (v 13). Do you hear the voice of God, longing for you to listen to him, yearning for you to enter into the fullness of life with him that Christ has given so much to obtain?

God lays out before the people a vision of what would happen if they 'would only listen' to him (vs 8,13). He would quickly 'subdue their enemies' (v 14) and they would be fed with 'the finest of wheat' and honey from wild bees (v 16), echoing the song of Moses.[3] Ultimately, however, God wants his people to be motivated not by what he can do for them but simply by who he is: 'I am the LORD your God' (v 10).

Come before God in silence. Thank him for Jesus' love and his sacrifice. Recommit yourself to listen to his voice.

---

[1] George Matheson, 1842–1906 [2] Beth Tanner, *The Book of Psalms*, Eerdmans, 2014, p639 [3] Deut 32:13

BIBLE IN A YEAR: **Exodus 23,24; Matthew 26**

1 Thessalonians 2:1–12

Seeking to Please

'Thine be the glory, risen conquering Son!'[1]

Those of us who preach or teach (on matters of faith or otherwise) have a difficult line to tread. We want to persuade our congregations or audiences, and so use language and techniques that will make our message appealing – but is there a danger that we slide into trying to impress our listeners mainly because it makes us feel good? Persuading others can be addictive. It seems that Paul himself may have been accused of preaching to the Thessalonians in order to bolster his status. He repeatedly defends himself from suggestions that he has been trying to please them, trick them, use flattery, or look for praise (vs 3–6).

What's the antidote to this temptation? It comes in two parts. First, focusing on serving and loving others for their sake can shift our attention away from our own desire for glory – or, in Paul's case, demonstrate that we are not self-motivated. Paul delightfully uses idealised images of parenthood to describe how he cared for the Thessalonians, nurturing them like a nursing mother (v 7b) and training them up like a father 'encouraging, comforting and urging [his children] to live lives worthy of God' (v 12). He completes the family portrait in saying that he also acted like an infant among them (v 7a), in refraining from asserting his authority. (Note that some manuscripts replace 'young children' with 'gentle' – there is only one letter between them in the Greek.[2]) Second, remember that God knows our innermost desires, more closely than we know them ourselves. Coming daily before God, who 'tests our hearts' (v 4), is the best way to uncover those self-serving motivations that subtly creep into our lives. God is the only audience that we rightly seek to please. May we ever seek to glorify him, not ourselves.

Are you trying to please God in your life, or people (v 4)? Ask the Holy Spirit to uncover what is in your heart.

---

[1] Edmond Budry, 1854–1932, tr Richard Birch Hoyle, 1875–1939
[2] Furnish, *Thessalonians*, Abingdon, 2007, p56–58

BIBLE IN A YEAR: **Exodus 25,26; Matthew 27**

Energised by the Word

Lord of life, may your word accomplish what you desire and achieve the purpose for which you sent it.[1]

I'm responsible for our household laundry. Frequently, I have to use a stain remover for blotches of tea, blood or chocolate. The instructions are to spray the stain and let it work. This reminds me of Paul's description of the Word of God being 'at work' in you who believe (v 13). The phrase is used throughout the New Testament to refer to God's activity among people and it's from a related Greek noun that we get the English word 'energy'.[2] It's amazing that the words we read in Scripture or hear preached can become 'the Word of God' to us, acting with energy and power to transform our lives and open our hearts to his truth. A friend recently described to me how he came to faith, hearing a preacher describe Jesus as like a parachute, saving him from falling. Through those human words, my friend heard and received the Word of God, which transformed his whole perception and life.

God's Word was 'at work' in the Thessalonians as well. First, like my friend, they turned to 'the living and true God'.[3] Second, they received gifts of faith, love and hope in Christ, which emerged in their work and endurance.[4] Third, they suffered persecution (v 14). (Paul digresses in verses 14–16 to criticise the Jews for persecuting the Judean churches and so trying to derail God's plan for salvation; this language doesn't license anti-Semitism, however – Paul loved his people and longed for them to accept Christ.)[5] Do you find it challenging that Paul considers the Thessalonians' suffering to be evidence of God's word working in them? This is no prosperity gospel. Much of the church, then and now, has discovered that, when God's activity meets opposition, persecution is often the result.

How has God's Word transformed your life, through the words of the Bible or other people? Pray that God will be at work through your words to others.

---

[1] From Isa 55:11 [2] Green, *Thessalonians*, Apollos, 2002, p140 [3] 1 Thess 1:9 [4] 1 Thess 1:3 [5] See Rom 9:3

BIBLE IN A YEAR: **Exodus 27,28; Matthew 28**

1 Thessalonians 3

Communicating Comfort

May we 'live a life of love, just as Christ loved us and gave himself up for us'.[1]

Many of us have known sadness at being unable to see loved ones during the Covid pandemic. It's particularly difficult when we know they're alone, or sick, and we feel helpless to support them. Paul is equally frustrated at being unable to visit the Thessalonians. Having heard about the persecution they are suffering, he is deeply concerned to know whether their newborn faith is surviving. He needn't have worried – Timothy reports that that their faith and love are standing up well (v 6).

What are our strategies for supporting one another in the faith, particularly when we can't be with one another all the time? Paul takes several steps to help the Thessalonians. Before leaving, he made sure that they were prepared to suffer persecution (vs 3,4). Do we sometimes paint an unrealistically rosy picture of the Christian life to potential or new converts? If so, their faith may not withstand the challenges that inevitably come. Then, once he is absent from the Thessalonians, Paul sends Timothy to 'strengthen and encourage' them in their faith (v 2) – and, of course, he writes this letter, which is full of love and encouragement. How can we creatively communicate with our fellow brothers and sisters in Christ when we're apart from them, whether these are housebound people in our local communities, or other Christians throughout the world?

Joyfully, Paul's relationship with the Thessalonians is far from one-sided. Just as he seeks to build them up, so he himself is greatly encouraged by their faith, in the midst of his own afflictions (v 7). Knowing that they are 'standing firm in the Lord' brings him life and joy (vs 8,9): he overflows with love for them (v 12). As we seek to support others in the Lord, may we, too, find our faith and joy refreshed.

Is there someone you feel led to encourage in the faith today?

---

[1] Eph 5:2

BIBLE IN A YEAR: Exodus 29,30; Psalm 18

Holy, Holy, Holy

Almighty God, Father, Son and Holy Spirit, be glorified in my heart and in my life.

For Paul, Christian faith is never a matter purely of what to believe; it is also a matter of how to 'live a holy life' (v 7). In his view, not to do so is to reject God, just as surely as not believing in him would be (v 8). Most of Paul's instructions in this passage relate to holiness in sexual relations. Given that sexual activity featured in pagan rituals, it's understandable that the apostles made it explicit to new converts that they needed to act in a holy and honourable way, not taking advantage of fellow believers (vs 3–6).[1] Had Paul been writing today, he might have stressed complying with safeguarding procedures to ensure that all in our communities are safe and no one is exploited. How does your church or community ensure that your common life is 'holy'?

For Paul, holiness isn't just a matter of good relationships. The Thessalonians' socio-economic lives must also be honourable. Paul's injunctions to 'lead a quiet life' and 'mind your own business' (v 11) might seem to imply that Christians shouldn't be extroverts or get involved in public debates. However, this would be to misconstrue his aim. It's possible that Paul was instead encouraging the Thessalonians to disengage from the patronage system, under which clients were paid by patrons (on whom they were economically dependent) to honour them in public discourse.[2] He urges them to support themselves in ways more likely to 'win the respect' of non-believers (v 12) and ensure that they aren't beholden to other people in how they speak and act. What might be equivalent ways of living for us today, that neither bring our faith into disrepute nor compromise our ability to live in accordance with our faith?

Paul acknowledges that the Thessalonians are already living lives pleasing to God, but encourages them to do so 'more and more' (vs 1,10). What more can you do?

---

[1] Green, *Thessalonians*, Apollos, 2002, p187 [2] Green, p210

BIBLE IN A YEAR: **Exodus 31,32; Acts 1**

1 Thessalonians 4:13–18

Welcome, Lord!

'... I am convinced that neither death nor life ... will be able to separate us from the love of God that is in Christ Jesus our Lord.'[1]

I was shocked and upset to learn recently that a close friend had been diagnosed with terminal cancer. A mutual friend said she was 'praying that her days will be filled with transfiguring grace' – beautiful words, which helped me, despite my grief, to see my dying friend as a dearly loved child of God who awaited the glorious culmination of her redemption in Christ.

Often, we need others to remind us that the grief we feel for loved ones who have died is not the final word and that there is a greater perspective. This seems to be Paul's role here. We can infer from this passage that the Thessalonians are grieving for some brothers and sisters who have recently died and that they are concerned that they will miss Jesus' eagerly anticipated return. Paul reassures them that those who have 'fallen asleep' in Christ (a common euphemism for death)[2] will rise when the Lord comes, to meet him together with those who remain living (v 17). The word Paul uses for Jesus' coming (*parousia* – v 15) was commonly used to refer to a magnificent imperial visit to a city, whose officials and people would travel outside the city to welcome the dignitary with great celebration.[3] All in Christ – whether living or dead – will rise to greet the Lord upon his return.

Some of the imagery Paul employs – the cry of command, the voice of the archangel, the trumpet call and the clouds (vs 16,17) – might seem slightly outlandish, but Paul is using it to paint a picture of the splendour and brilliance of the Lord's return, as our divine and rightful sovereign. His aim is less to outline the logistics of the second coming than to evoke excitement at the prospect of welcoming Christ in all his glory – along with all our beloved sisters and brothers.

Pray that God will increase in you the gift of hope in Christ. Come, Lord Jesus, come!

---

[1] Rom 8:38,39 [2] Witherington, *Thessalonians*, Eerdmans, 2006, p131 [3] Witherington, p138

BIBLE IN A YEAR: **Exodus 33,34; Acts 2**

Steady as You Go

'The LORD is my light and my salvation – whom shall I fear? The LORD is the stronghold of my life – of whom shall I be afraid?'[1]

I'm intrigued by the behaviour of some motorists on a stretch of road near where I live. They speed where there are no speed cameras, slow down to pass the camera, and then speed up again. I wonder, if the cameras were hidden, if the bad drivers would be caught and others encouraged to comply with the speed limit consistently.

Paul might be unfamiliar with this illustration, but he would definitely understand the psychology behind it. He resists any pressure to speculate about specific 'times and dates' of the day of judgement (v 1), observing that the day of the Lord (like a hidden camera) will arrive unexpectedly, as Jesus made clear in his own teaching.[2] Unbelievers (like speeding drivers) might assume that the system doesn't apply to them, but they will certainly be caught (v 3). On the other hand, believers, like the Thessalonians, need not worry about being caught out. They are children of light, chosen not to 'suffer wrath' but to 'receive salvation' through Jesus Christ (v 9). Their whole lives are preparation for the final day, as they walk in accordance with their calling. They are like the consistently careful drivers.

There is both encouragement and challenge for us in Paul's message. Whatever our circumstances or however we feel, we can have confidence that we do not 'belong to the night' (v 5), but to Christ. He has saved you – and that's a fact! But there's also a challenge. Does the whole of your life reflect your identity as a child of light, or are there parts which lurk in the shadows, lacking in faith, love or hope? Take heart: according to Paul, we can 'put on' these virtues that are our spiritual inheritance, just as a soldier 'puts on' a breastplate, or helmet (see v 8). What do you need to put on today?

Imagine this is your last day, week or month of life. How might this change how you live?

[1] Ps 27:1 [2] Matt 24:36; Mark 13:32

BIBLE IN A YEAR: Exodus 35,36; Psalm 19

An Almighty Assembly

'The Son is the image of the invisible God ... all things have been created through him and for him.'[1]

Why is the first commandment, 'You shall have no other gods before me'?[2] Presumably because the Israelites were in danger of becoming attracted to other gods. Israel was a small nation surrounded by larger and more powerful cultures whose established religions were thoroughly polytheistic. The Hebrew prophets resist this worldview by asserting God's role as Sovereign Creator and denouncing other gods as worthless idols.[3]

This psalm takes a different tack. The psalmist plays on the ancient Near Eastern idea of the gods meeting in assembly under the presidency of a supreme god, to decide what would happen on earth.[4] Here, however, God himself is presiding, gathering the other gods around him to judge them for their complete failures in just leadership. They have acted in the interest of the 'unjust'

and 'wicked', instead of defending the 'weak and the fatherless ... the poor and the oppressed' (vs 2,3). Consequently – in a shock departure from ancient Near Eastern mythologies – God effectively strips these gods of their divine status, decreeing that they will 'die like mere mortals' (v 7). At the end, the psalmist calls on God himself to restore justice on earth, as its true and rightful ruler (v 8).

Despite the psalm's purported setting, we are right to hear God's criticisms of the gods (vs 2–4) as directed also at those who have leadership responsibilities on earth. In later Judaism the 'gods' were interpreted as referring to the Jewish people (as Jesus' comments in John 10:34-36 indicate).[5] Can we respond by reflecting on how we measure up to this moral commission today, as well as joining the psalmist in urging God to 'rise up' and bring justice to all the nations (v 8)?

Reflect on these words from Micah 6:8: '... what does the LORD require of you? To act justly and to love mercy and to walk humbly with your God.'

---

[1] Col 1:15,16 [2] Exod 20:3 [3] Eg Isa 44:6-20 [4] Robert Davidson, *The Vitality of Worship*, Handsel, 1998, p271 [5] Mays, *Psalms*, John Knox, 1994, p270

BIBLE IN A YEAR: **Exodus 37,38; Acts 3**

1 Thessalonians 5:12–28

We are the Church

'O most merciful redeemer, friend and brother, may I know thee more clearly, love thee more dearly, and follow thee more nearly, day by day.'[1]

A fellow church leader recently complained to me that his congregation seemed to expect him to drive everything they did as a church. They were (usually) happy to turn up Sunday by Sunday, but didn't see it as their responsibility to do much else.

Paul paints a very different picture of what church is like. Yes, the church leadership is described as 'those who work hard among you' (v 12) – but most of his instructions here are addressed to 'all the brothers and sisters' in the church, to whom he expressly requires his letter to be read (v 27). It is these normal Christians who are urged to maintain pastoral responsibility for one another, warning those who are 'idle and disruptive', encouraging the disheartened, helping the weak and striving always 'to do what is good' for those in and outside the church (vs 14,15). Do you, or does your church, need to rediscover this commission? We are, above all, a community of people in Christ, building up our common life in mutual peace (vs 13,14). We need leadership and we are to recognise those who are leaders among us and lovingly respect them (vs 12,13), but this does not exempt us from our responsibilities as a body. It seems likely that this was core teaching the apostles gave to new faith communities, as it is paralleled elsewhere.[2]

Maybe this ideal feels unattainable for you at the moment? Be encouraged: our collective growth in Christian maturity is not solely our responsibility – above all, it is God's! Paul prays that God himself will 'sanctify you through and through' (v 23 – the Greek 'you' is plural). Having called us, God enables us to grow, right up to the end (vs 23,24). And 'he will do it' (v 24)!

'... encourage one another and build each other up, just as in fact you are doing' (v 11).

---

[1] Prayer of Richard of Chichester, 1197–1253 [2] Rom 12:3–21; Green, *Thessalonians*, Apollos, 2002, p246

BIBLE IN A YEAR: **Exodus 39,40; Acts 4**

2 Thessalonians 1

Just Judgement

God our teacher and our guide, may your word be a 'lamp to my feet and a light for my path.'[1]

Does this passage make you feel uncomfortable, with its apocalyptic imagery of 'everlasting destruction' (v 9)? Before we look more closely at it, acknowledge your feelings honestly to God and pray again the prayer above.

I hope most of us never experience the persecution and suffering the Thessalonian Christians endured, but if we did – or do – it's easier to understand why Paul might be concerned to assure them that God would come and bring justice on earth. They might easily have started wondering: are we suffering because God has rejected us? Or forgotten us? Philosophical debate at the time was questioning the idea of divine judgement.[2] Accordingly, Paul acts swiftly to reassure the Thessalonians that their perseverance under suffering is evidence that they are 'worthy of the kingdom of God' (v 5) and that God in Jesus Christ will not fail to bring them justice and relief on the day he comes in glory. It's important to read the references to punishment in this light. Paul's focus is on 'those who trouble' the Thessalonians (v 6) receiving their just punishment. For 'God will never forget the needy; the hope of the afflicted will never perish'.[3] For God to be good and loving, he must be just.

In 2020, Mina Smallman's daughters were murdered in London. She strove for justice. Yet she also spoke of her ability to forgive the killer as being God's gift, enabling her to be free.[4] We are able to hold these responses together because the Lord Jesus, who brings justice for the afflicted, is also the one who died upon the cross. Jesus leads the Thessalonians, and us, in enduring suffering with faith. We trust in him, not ourselves, for salvation and ultimate justice.

Pray: God, make us worthy of your calling. By your power, bring to fruition our every desire for goodness and every deed prompted by faith (v 11).

---

[1] Ps 119:105, TNIV [2] Green, *Thessalonians*, Apollos, 2002, p293 [3] Ps 9:18
[4] BBC Radio 4, *Today*, 1 January 2022

BIBLE IN A YEAR: **Leviticus 1–3; Acts 5**

Doomed to Destruction

'Blessed are those who make the Lord their trust, who do not look to the proud, to those who turn aside to false gods.'[1]

It's easy to be misled by appearances. My friend uses an old disinfectant bottle to spray her house plants with water. One day, she unwittingly picked up the real disinfectant – which looked identical – and sprayed a begonia with it!

Evil can also be deceptive and harmful. We don't know exactly what Paul means by the coming 'man of lawlessness' (v 3) who will set himself up 'in God's temple' (v 4), though it seems likely that he may have been inspired by the Roman emperor Augustus, for whom a temple was built in Thessalonica as part of his imperial cult.[2] However, it is clear that this 'man' symbolises everything that is utterly opposed to faith – while presenting himself as something to be worshipped. All the way through this passage, Paul describes this 'lawless one' by using language that he normally uses only about God and Christ: he is 'revealed' (vs 3,8); his power is 'secret' (v 7, the word used is the same Paul uses for the 'mystery' of God in various letters);[3] he is 'at work' (v 7); he is 'coming' (v 9). Yet it is all a lie. Paul says that the power of lawlessness is 'already at work' (v 7). Can you identify people or things around you that deceive others into thinking they are worthy of worship?

We might be concerned about being misled ourselves by Satan's deceptions. However, Paul describes the ones who are deceived as those 'who refused to love the truth' (v 10), not those who have accepted it. (My friend soon realised her mistake and the plant survived!) Paul's message for the Thessalonians is to 'remember' what he has told them before (v 5). We also have nothing to fear from the enemy, while we hold on to the gospel truth that we have received.

Pray for the Lord's mercy towards unbelieving friends and family.

---

[1] Ps 40:4, TNIV [2] Green, *Thessalonians*, Apollos, 2002, p310–312 [3] Eg Eph 3:3,4,9; Col 1:26,27; see Green, p317.

BIBLE IN A YEAR: **Leviticus 4,5; Psalms 20,21**

2 Thessalonians 2:13 – 3:5

Pedal Pals

'We love because he first loved us.'[1]

I've recently discovered the benefits of an electric bike. People ask me if it does all the work, like an electric scooter, but in fact you do have to pedal – your pedalling and the electrical assistance work in symbiosis to get you around.

There are similarities with Paul's description of the work of salvation in verse 13. This involves some human pedalling: the Christian must decide to believe in the truth. Some gospel presentations seem to suggest that this decision is the only requirement, but look more closely: Paul says that the Thessalonians are saved not because they believed, but through their belief. The reason they are saved is because God chose them, the first in their region (the 'firstfruits' of a harvest were the first produce, dedicated to God).[2] God's choice is not arbitrary, but is intrinsically connected with his love for them.

Paul does not speculate on why they were chosen as opposed to others: rather, he gives thanks that they are loved and chosen to be saved. Can we follow his example? There is no more tangible display of God's love for us than Christ hanging on the cross. We are not party to the mysteries of God's working, but we can respond in belief and thanksgiving.

There is another aspect to salvation. The Thessalonians were saved not only through their belief, but through 'the sanctifying work of the Spirit' – in other words, by the Holy Spirit working in them to make them holy. This implies that Paul views salvation not as a one-off event, but as a continuing process. Again, this is a process which requires our pedalling – Paul urges the Thessalonians to 'stand firm' and 'hold fast' to his teaching (v 15) – but is empowered by God, who strengthens us 'in every good deed and word' (v 17).

Paul was also involved in the Thessalonians' salvation in that they were 'called … through our gospel' (v 14). Who is God calling you to?

---

[1] 1 John 4:19 [2] Green, *Thessalonians*, Apollos, 2002, p326

BIBLE IN A YEAR: **Leviticus 6,7; Acts 6**

Working Witness

'May the Lord direct your hearts into God's love and Christ's perseverance.'[1]

It can be tempting to adopt a rose-tinted view of the early church, but it's clear that even among the exemplary Thessalonians there were some who refused to comply with the apostles' teaching and example (vs 6,9). How would you advise the church to deal with this situation? In Paul's view, the time for gentle persuasion is past. He urges such people to comply (v 12) and commands the rest of the Thessalonians to avoid them (though not to excommunicate them altogether), to shame them into realising that their behaviour is wrong (vs 6,14,15). However, before we unquestioningly adopt similar tactics in our communities today, it's worth reflecting on potential differences between the Thessalonians' culture and our own.

In first-century Mediterranean societies, the honour of belonging to the social group, and the shame of exclusion, were powerful motivations for people's behaviour,[2] but today, certainly in Western cultures, shaming someone is usually a blunt and cruel instrument for changing their behaviour, more likely to lead to hurt or further antagonism than to redemption. What tactics do you think might be more appropriate or effective?

The nature of the insubordination among the Thessalonians is a refusal to work (v 10). It seems unlikely that this was connected with their belief in Jesus' imminent coming, or Paul would surely have addressed that issue here.[3] More plausibly, they have become reliant on donations from patrons, busying themselves on their behalf in the public assembly and failing to earn their own food.[4] We cannot extrapolate from this that manual labour is somehow more Christian than working in politics, for example, but we might reflect: is the way I spend my time, whether paid or not, honouring to God and to others?

Prayerfully, reflect over the next few weeks on how you use your time. Do you feel called to make any changes?

---

[1] 2 Thess 3:5 [2] Green, *Thessalonians*, Apollos, 2002, p355 [3] Furnish, *Thessalonians*, Abingdon, 2007, p177 [4] Green, p351

BIBLE IN A YEAR: **Leviticus 8,9; Acts 7**

WHEN IN ROME...

Jesus lived and died, and the church was born, against the background of the Roman Empire, and some knowledge of that context helps us to understand the New Testament. The origins of Rome are lost in myth and legend, but what is certain is that a small village on the banks of the Tiber became, in the space of something under a thousand years and through a mix of conquest, alliance and annexation, a centre of power, controlling territory stretching from Britain to Syria and from Germany to North Africa.

Until 27 BC Rome was a republic, governed by the Senate drawn from leading citizens, but at this point the empire was instituted and control passed to the emperor. The vast empire was governed in different ways. In some areas – especially the more volatile, those on the borders or those with a recent history of insurrection – Rome ruled directly through a governor appointed by the emperor, for example Pilate in Judea during Jesus' ministry. Others were governed by a puppet king such as Herod the Great at the time of Jesus' birth or Herod Antipas in Galilee during Jesus' ministry.

Control was exercised through a combination of military might, political and legal administration, and taxation.

Roman legions were deployed in border regions or troubled areas; elsewhere local auxiliaries were raised. Political administration depended to a large extent on local authorities. Taxation took three forms – land tax, poll tax and customs duties. The first two were collected by local authorities, the last by the tax collectors we meet in the Gospels. These were 'tax farmers' who bought the right to collect the taxes. To show a return on their investment, they often charged over the rate.

An empire of this size required significant infrastructure. Roman roads were designed to enable the legions to reach areas of trouble rapidly and they became key routes of communication and an important factor in the spread of the gospel. Trade in food, goods, weapons and slaves was conducted by road and by ships on the Mediterranean, means of transport used by Paul and his associates. A common language, Koine Greek, which had been widely adopted following the conquests of Alexander the Great, facilitated trade and the communication of the gospel.

Roman society was highly stratified, with little social mobility. The upper classes, comprising about one per cent of the population, controlled nearly all property and resources. The rest – including slaves, the owners of small businesses and farms, and casual labourers – had little economic security and were disadvantaged by a legal system that favoured the rich and powerful. They were often obliged to seek patronage from the better off. In return for financial benefit from the patron, the client would be expected to boost the patron's honour by extolling the patron's virtues. In some cases, the patron might sponsor a business venture and so receive not only honour but economic benefit. Sometimes a broker or mediator might bring patron and client together and facilitate the relationship.

The patron-client system was a key building block of Roman society and its language, in which the patron shows favour or grace (Greek, *charis*) and the recipient responds with gratitude and respect. This is reflected in the New Testament description of God's relationship with his people through Christ. At the same time the free nature of the gospel and the equality of status which it brought challenged the economic and social dependency of the system.

Patrons gained honour through their benefactions. Honour, which was highly desired and the motivating force for much behaviour, depended on the approval of society and on displaying the values of the group and demonstrating loyalty to the group. Dishonour or shame arose when the values were contravened. Early Christians were often seen to be bringing shame on their communities – an idea which persists in some cultures – and this brought opposition. Strands of New Testament teaching suggest that following a crucified Saviour, far from being a mark of shame as most perceived it, was a badge of honour.[1]

Women, for the most part, did not play a prominent role in society, although Roman women enjoyed a greater freedom than their Greek or Jewish counterparts and had considerable authority in the home. Some had prominent roles in religious cults. They did not hold political power, although wives of prominent politicians might exercise influence, as did Pilate's wife. While most trades and professions were largely executed by men there were exceptions: Lydia was a wealthy businesswoman and Phoebe is described as a benefactor (NIV) or patron (ESV).[2] There is evidence that in the first century some women were causing concern by becoming more assertive and flouting traditional norms. This, combined with the new status that Jesus

[1] Eg Rom 1:16; Heb 12:2; 13:13 [2] Rom 16:1,2

gave women, may have led to certain misunderstandings and tensions at the time and to later misreadings of the New Testament.

Slaves formed a key part of the economy, performing all the menial tasks and many of the more demanding ones. Those on large agricultural estates or in the mines (extracting iron for weapons, tin and copper for utensils) had the worst roles. Domestic slaves might fill professional roles such as teaching or estate management and could rise to positions of some influence, but they had no rights and were often subject to physical and sexual abuse. Estimates of the numbers vary, but across the empire it may have been around ten per cent of the population, rising to nearer thirty per cent in some urban areas. Slaves were obtained through warfare, natural reproduction, kidnapping or the taking-in of unwanted infants discarded on rubbish dumps.

The names in the New Testament suggest that many of the early Christians were slaves, although others were owners of houses large enough to accommodate meetings of Christians. Some slaves might be granted freedom by their owners, perhaps as a reward for faithful service over many years. The gospel cut across the differentiation between slave and owner, abolishing status distinctions, as Philemon had to discover. Both Paul and Jesus used the language of slavery as a metaphor for aspects of Christian life. Later forms of slavery differed in some respects; ethnicity, for example, was not a feature of slavery in the ancient world.

The Romans did not fully share the Greeks' love for philosophical debate, but the Greek philosophical schools had adherents: we meet the Stoics and the Epicureans in Acts[3] and Paul challenges the sophistry of Greek thought in 1 Corinthians. The art of rhetoric was highly valued by both Romans and Greeks and its principles have influenced the way in which some New Testament arguments are presented.

Popular entertainment took the form of the theatre (where the great age of Greek drama had been replaced by farce and sexual innuendo), athletics and chariot races, as well as the bloodthirsty and violent gladiatorial and wild-animal contests in the arena – which were often used to deal with perceived criminal elements or subversives.

[3] Acts 17:18

Education was both formal and informal. Literacy rates were relatively high, with most children receiving an elementary education. Upper-class males proceeded to higher levels, being trained in medicine, law, philosophy or rhetoric.

Religion was an important unifying factor. Greek and Roman pantheons mirrored one another and it was expected that all citizens would be involved in the worship of the gods; failure to do so was seen as a mark of disloyalty. Other religions, such as Judaism and local cults, were tolerated to varying degrees. Mystery religions, so called, were popular and offered secret enlightenment to the initiated. In contrast, Paul declares that the mystery of God's plan of salvation has been revealed to all.

From the time of Augustus (27 BC – AD 41) there was a tendency to see the emperor as divine, initially after death and even, later, during his lifetime, leading to a growing emperor cult, especially in the east of the empire. This led to conflict between the church and the authorities towards the end of the New Testament period and into the second century. The insistence of Christians that Jesus was Lord – and, by implication, that Caesar was not – meant that they were seen as subversive.

The early church developed in an era of totalitarian and often unsympathetic government. It was willing to exploit the benefits provided by the system in so far as they served the cause of the gospel, but when beliefs and values conflicted, the Christians would not compromise. Perhaps relationships between the Christian community and political power always have similar ambiguity. In the small group I led at an international conference on the Bible in 1994, there were two people from the Philippines: one Catholic and one Protestant. We learned that, at the time of the Philippine revolution, the Protestant pastors argued from Romans 13 that the Aquino government should be respected, whereas Catholic priests invoked Revelation 13 to argue that the state was corrupt and must be opposed. Early Christians, while determined to live as good citizens so far as was possible, recognised that their ultimate citizenship was elsewhere: that is what determined their values and lifestyle. In that we, today, are no different.

FOR FURTHER READING
Everett Ferguson, *Backgrounds of Early Christianity*, Eerdmans, 2003
Mary Beard, *SPQR*, Profile Books, 2015

INTRODUCTION
Hosea

LIVING GOD'S MESSAGE IN DARK TIMES

The book of Hosea is generally not one of the most popular books in the Bible. It contains a prophetic voice that is largely condemnatory. However, scattered throughout we find that there are verses of great hope that point towards God's grace and, for us, towards Jesus' earthly ministry and his second coming. The opening verse tells us that Hosea prophesied during the reign of certain kings in the eighth century BC. Therefore, his ministry would have crossed over with that of Isaiah, although their focus was different. We find that Hosea mostly prophesied to the wayward northern tribes of Israel, frequently referring to Ephraim. The use of this word was either an expression for northern Israel or, specifically, for the tribe of the same name.

God's message through Hosea is largely composed of warnings of the fulfilment of judgement resulting from the idolatry of the people. God's covenant with Israel, made at Sinai, had been broken so frequently by Israel that they were now going to pay the consequences. During the middle of Hosea's ministry, two and a half tribes were exiled by Assyria; the rest of Israel would follow on soon enough. The prophecies and ensuing exile also served as warnings to Judah, who, a century later, would face similar judgement. It is no surprise, then, that the contents of Hosea's prophecies are mostly condemnatory.

Central to the opening chapters is an analogy of redemption in God's command to Hosea in his marriage and parenthood. These lived-out prophecies point the original audience towards their sin and God's invitation to repent, while they point us to our continuing need of Jesus. Hosea had to find a way to live amongst a rebellious people, including his wife, and we are challenged to read this in a responsive way. I would suggest that an appropriate response will be centred around thanksgiving, worship and repentance. May God's Spirit inspire the devotional reading of this book.

Jamys Carter

What's in a Name?

Pause and be still. Rest a while before God. Ask God to speak into your life through his words. Be prepared to be challenged and encouraged by his Spirit.

Like some of the other prophets, Hosea is called to demonstrate the message of God through more than just words. This passage tells of his call to marry a promiscuous woman and of their subsequent children. In many cultures, the naming of children is a powerful and significant event, full of meaning. The idea of a 'Christian' name stems from the renaming of the likes of Simon (Peter) and Saul (Paul). Hosea's children are given meanings that relate to the culture and crisis of their day.

All my life I have had to explain my first name. It is a rare Celtic name that I pronounce as James, but I have no idea if that is what it originally sounded like; I regularly receive a variety of attempts to make sense of the letters. For me, in my Western culture, my name has only minor significance, I just want it spelt and pronounced correctly. I am not all that bothered by what the name means (I can't even remember). Rather, I want to be known by what I do and to whom I belong: God.

Hosea's children were given names that had prophetic meanings. Whenever they were spoken about, the meaning would be inferred. God's message through Hosea was a message of inclusion and grace, despite all that the people had done. Rejecting God is to reject his love and his invitation into his family. To accept God is to receive his grace-gift of love and adoption into his worldwide family. Who we are, as Christians, is found in who God is and who he says we are. That may be evident in our name, or in the name he gave us: children of God.[1]

How does the message of being adopted, based upon grace and faith, challenge how you look at the way other people live?

[1] John 1:12

BIBLE IN A YEAR: **Leviticus 10–12; Psalm 22**

Psalm 83

God Speaks in the Silence

Start with a time of total quiet. Then pray that God will allow love and grace to flow through you as you soak in biblical promises today.

The heart cry of this psalm is for God to bring a judgement against those who are plotting against Israel. Although Asaph lists some of the historic enemies of Israel, whom he is using to compare with the current threats, the psalm starts with a heart-rending cry. It is here that we can pause and find encouragement. God, the silent one? The deaf one? The aloof one? Can we even say or think such things of the Word, the all-hearing, the ever-present one? Yet here, in this psalm, we can find permission and solace with such a thought.

There have been many times in my life when I have wanted an answer from God. Times when I have felt that many of my personal prayers were being left unanswered. Now I know that God does hear and that God does answer, even if the answer is 'no' or 'later' – but waiting in silence can be so hard. I am thankful that the psalms are full of examples of people who speak out their frustrated emotions, knowing that God is big enough and gracious enough to take it.

When Elijah was finally given a chance to encounter God, it was in the silence that God spoke.[1] Although God can speak to us in the noisy times ('Deep calls to deep in the roar of your waterfalls'),[2] there are times when we need to come to a place of quiet, both internally and externally, to hear the voice of the Spirit. Above all, we cling to the promises of God's Word in the Bible, the promises that God is with us and for us, remembering that it is only through a test that we have a testimony.

Explore different ways of approaching God in your devotions, perhaps borrowing from other Christian traditions. Expect God to meet you as you draw near in faithfulness.

[1] 1 Kings 19:12 [2] Ps 42:7

BIBLE IN A YEAR: **Leviticus 13,14; Acts 8**

Restorative Love

Ever-loving Father, open my eyes to the blessings you have for me this day. May I walk in openness before you.

God's message through Hosea in this passage reminds us of the great restoration that God has for the whole world. Hosea demonstrated this love and grace by buying back his unfaithful wife, restoring her into a loving marriage. It is almost unfathomable to imagine a pure and holy God having such grace towards sinners, and yet that is the gospel. Despite Gomer's lack of voice here (we don't know how repentant she was), God's grace is restorative: through Jesus all who are repentant find grace and mercy.

My memories of when I first became a Christian are filled with exciting times of corporate worship, expectant prayer meetings and instructive Bible teaching. I was eager and open to God. Many years on, I am challenged to remain eager and open to all that God has for me, but I am mature enough now to know that my Christian walk goes through seasons, some of which bring considerable challenge, whereas others offer time to rest and restore.

As Paul reminds us, Hosea's message refers to the whole world, not just the Jews.[1] God's love for the Israelites, despite their frequent sins, is a foretaste of the grace we find in Jesus. Jesus has sought us and bought us, we are invited back into a family of love, into a place where we are accepted despite our past, into a place where we are included and where we matter. The love of God restores us to something more than we had. We now have a God-given hope: we are not just given a new start – we are given eternal life, a life hidden in Christ. God has done so much for us to live in this restoration. Let's enter more fully into that each day.

Be comforted and encouraged by the good news we have received. Pray with thanksgiving for God's amazing grace and bountiful mercy. Accept with faith the restoration he offers.

[1] Rom 9:25

BIBLE IN A YEAR: **Leviticus 15,16; Acts 9**

Hosea 4:1 – 5:7

Knowing God's Way

Holy Spirit, may you search me and show me those areas that you want to transform in me. Help me to hear and obey, for your glory.

Priests, prophets and people, all come under the microscope of God's judgement in this passage – not that God needs a microscope to see their sins! Their sins are public and promoted, visible like an advertising billboard or targeted internet advertising. Much like the example of Gomer that we read about earlier, promiscuity has become the norm. As we learn elsewhere, however, God cannot be mocked: we reap what we sow.[1]

It is sometimes easier to blame the influencers we follow than to take responsibility for our own lives. Bad leaders may be aplenty in the world, but we cannot hide our own mistakes by blaming them. Before I made a commitment to follow Jesus, I called myself a Christian but I took a piecemeal approach to accepting the teachings of the Bible. It was easy enough to find a church or a leader who would not have challenged my self-serving lifestyle. In truly choosing to follow Christ, however, I was faced with my own failings and had to start a process of repentance. Like Hosea's audience, I could no longer blame a lack of knowledge.

God's challenge to us is not just to follow some teaching or leader, but to know God personally. We need to be able to give a reason for the choices we make, not just to others but to ourselves and ultimately to God. Judgement is not limited to the Old Testament, as some try to claim. Rather, right at the heart of the cross, where we meet grace and mercy, we also see wrath and judgement. The message of the gospel is centred around Jesus taking our judgement. That is the foundation from which we must live. Now that is the kind of knowledge that we must never lack!

Consider the influencers in your life: are they helping you to grow closer to God? Equally, be encouraged to be a positive influence to all you meet today.

[1] Gal 6:7

BIBLE IN A YEAR: **Leviticus 17,18; Acts 10**

Hosea 5:8 – 6:11a

Draw in Close to God

Loving Saviour, help me to know the cost of your love for me, that I may be able to cling to you and find the comfort you promise.

This passage reminds us, as followers of God, that when we are disciplined we must draw near to God rather than turn away and seek help elsewhere. Hosea's audience had rebelled against God and reaped the consequences. In their pain, they were now looking to find help from other nations. Those nations, however, could not offer the kind of help that the people needed. Running to God is always better than running from God.

There are plenty of examples in the Bible of people who try to run from God. Jonah is the classic example. No matter how far we go or how fast we think we are, God is always there. For us who love Jesus, the principal challenge we face revolves around our obedience to God's command and call. Jesus, who took our punishment, commands us to love and calls us to serve. However that love and service may manifest in your experience, there will be time when it hurts, costs and feels hopeless. It is at those times that we may choose to give up, in effect running away to others for comfort. It is here, however, in the hurt and the pain, that we find that our Saviour understands us perfectly.

Just as Hosea declares, with God there is healing, revival, restoration and an abiding presence. His listeners could have a hope that goes beyond their circumstances. We, today, have a hope too, one that looks back at the cross of Jesus and one that looks forward to our eternal experience; both the backward and forward hope help us to have a living hope today. That hope inspires us to press in close to God, no matter what we are feeling, and there we can find his healing, revival, restoration and presence.

Think about your community of faith. Are there people who currently need to hear this message of hope? How can you show them this life of hope?

BIBLE IN A YEAR: **Leviticus 19,20; Psalms 23,24**

Holiness and Grace

Heavenly Father, help me to understand your holiness and your grace, that I may see Jesus at work in me and that I may grow in his image.

There is no doubt that we live in times that are similar to Hosea's. We may not be in Jerusalem or Israel, we may not be looking for help from Assyria or Egypt, but the underlying theme is the same. Here we read that the kings and princes 'delight' in the sins of the people (v 3). The word translated 'delight' is regularly used for 'rejoice'. So, the key leaders and influencers rejoice in the sins of the people and their response encourages continuing sin. We can imagine similar things being said about some influencers and leaders of our day – but, as Paul tells us, where sin abounds, grace abounds more.[1]

We often have to deal with the difficulty of living as Christians in the world. We are not called to remove ourselves but, like Jesus, to be friends of sinners.[2] However, as we reach out to those who do not know Jesus, we must make sure that we are neither approving of sin, nor sinning. While Jesus managed to find this balance, I have to work hard at keeping it: either I stay away from people, or I try to fit in by being similar. Jesus neither rejoiced in nor approved of sin; that is our guide.

As we see in our passage, God's heart is to redeem the people. In this instance they do not respond. There is only so much that Hosea can do. He has to deliver the message and let them respond. We too are called to be faithful in our witness of Jesus' grace in our lives. How people respond is ultimately up to them. Start with yourself and make sure that you are open to all that God has for you. Then, in faithfulness, demonstrate that, in all you say, think and do.

Consider the influencers of your life: are they encouraging you to grow in your faith? How are you influencing others? Can they see the grace of God through you?

[1] Rom 5:20, AV [2] Matt 11:19

BIBLE IN A YEAR: **Leviticus 21,22; Acts 11**

Responding to Holiness

Dear God, may your holiness inspire me to turn away from anything that is contrary to you. Shine your light through the Holy Spirit, into the depths of my heart.

Today's passage must have been deeply troubling to hear. At best, Hosea's audience were offering sacrifices and offerings, but these were devoid of the all-important right attitude. At worst, they were rebelling and rejecting all that is good, all that is from God. The people had chosen their own path: they made idols and appointed leaders without God's consent. All these sins would lead them into exile; Hosea's warnings would fall, largely, on deaf ears.

It's not easy to be told that you are wrong, nor that your lifestyle is wrong. As a pastor, some of the most challenging conversations I have ever had were with people in my congregation who were making sinful choices. It is a desperately hard thing to talk about. Jesus reminds us to take a good look at ourselves first, because it is always far easier to find fault in others. The choice to walk away from church and God can offer itself as an easier option than to admit fault and repent. However, it is often through the more challenging things that we grow.

Hosea's message did not lead to widespread repentance. That was not the fault of the messenger, nor of the message. Today we are able to point people to Jesus who, having given himself, forgives all who come with faith and repentance. Pointing people to Jesus is a fruitful way in which lives can be changed. It is far less my job to point out someone's fault; rather, the Holy Spirit, who lets me know when I need to repent, is able to guide others. Our lives should emulate the grace of Jesus, while acknowledging the incredible holiness of God. Let our words be salted with the healing and fragrance of the grace we have received.

Pray for those who have walked away from church and God. Pray that they may be drawn back and find hope in the community of faith.

BIBLE IN A YEAR: **Leviticus 23,24; Acts 12**

Hosea 9:10 – 10:15

Open to a Soaking

Holy Spirit, help me to be open to your promptings and leadings. Show me the way you want me to go. Lead me in life for your glory.

In today's reading, Hosea's message continues to highlight the historic and current sin that leads the people into God's judgement and their own destruction. Recurrent themes of idolatry, trusting in anything but God and generally being deceitful fill these words. Yet, all is not lost. Despite the consequences of sin, God still offers hope for those who turn to him. We read in 10:12 that the people could be showered with God's righteousness. The condition for this blessing is based upon their wholesale change: they must break the 'unploughed ground' (10:12) and return to living a life for God. For too long they have ignored God and done their own thing; Hosea's message gives them hope, as long as they change.

There are times in life when many will realise that they have been neglecting to live for God in some area. The unploughed ground may represent a lack of some spiritual practice like fasting, prayer, giving, hospitality – now being spotlighted by the Holy Spirit. To find fruitfulness in this area requires both work by us and work by God. We have to 'break up' the ground – the hard work to re-establish the practice. Once we have made the choice and set ourselves to the discipline, that is when God rains on us and the harvest comes. In practical terms, we need to set ourselves to the practice identified by the Holy Spirit and, as we do so, it is with God's help that we reap the benefit.

The emphasis of Hosea's message here does not suggest a high expectation of the people responding. That, of course, is their choice. Let us ensure that we have no 'unploughed ground' in our lives; rather, that we are open and receptive to the rain of the Holy Spirit.

Let us be open to the promptings of the Holy Spirit to consider if there is some area that we need to be working on to become more fruitful.

Transformational Weeping

Consider how God is near you today. Think of some of the ways in which you can know his presence with you. Now take some time to praise him.

What a lovely focus the psalmist brings here, desiring to be close to God and recognising the incomparable blessings that come from God. Yet, there is a cry of desperation in these words, for the sparrow and swallow have a home in the house of God, but the author writes as one who is far off, yearning to be closer to God's presence. The focus is on the pilgrim, the one who chooses to make the journey to come to Jerusalem, on this occasion through the dry valley of Baka. The word Baka is derived from the word to weep and the valley is sometimes referred to as the valley of weeping.

I once asked a dear Christian friend from India his views on alternative ways to share communion. Rather than enter into any controversy, he simply stated that whenever he approaches communion he approaches as one who is broken.

He sees the agony of the cross in direct response to his own life and is deeply thankful and broken for the gift of God. I am encouraged to return to this thought whenever I become too familiar with any aspect of my relationship with God.

I picture pilgrims coming through the valley with weeping, their tears soaking into the dry ground, making it a 'place of springs' (v 6). As we read elsewhere, 'Those who sow with tears will reap with songs of joy'.[1] Their journey leads them towards the presence of God, but the journey itself is transformational. Our walk with God can bring transformation through all the seasons we travel. Our weeping, our joy, our commute and our stillness can all bring transformation. Unlike those in the day of the psalmist, who travel to God's Temple, we ourselves are the temple of the Holy Spirit.

As presence bearers, consider how God can use you to be transformational in even the most barren of places. Be encouraged to know that God chooses to use the broken.

[1] Ps 126:5

BIBLE IN A YEAR: **Leviticus 27; Numbers 1; Acts 13**

Hosea 11:1–11

Steadfast Love

Father God, help me to see myself as you see me. Help me to wonder anew at your grace and mercy today.

In this chapter we are exposed to a God of tenderness, judgement and grace. As the historical interactions between God and Israel are given a brief overview, it is as if we are being given a picture of the inner working of God's reasoning. We are reminded how close God is. From calling Israel out of Egypt, to healing them; then, using the language of a parent to a toddler, by helping them to walk and lifting them up to embrace them. God is invested in Hosea's listeners – but they have been less invested in God, honouring with their lips but not their lives.

Dishonouring God can be an easy path to drift down. It is unlikely that we had such a destination in mind, but the pressures of life and the voices of the crowd can eat away at our faith commitment. God has been involved in our lives before we were even born. As we grew up, God was there. There would have been times in our lives when we were called or taken care of and we did not even know it. This is how it is with God: wherever we go, there God is. Just as Israel's sin needed judgement, so too did ours. The best response is at the altar of repentance: it is there that we find grace and mercy.

God's heart is clear in verse 8, where three times we read, 'How can I ...'. This is the love of a parent who has given so much, has been broken in the process, but still wants to give more. This is fulfilled in Jesus, the true Son who was called out of Egypt.[1] It is in Jesus that we see the pain that our sin has caused, yet he demonstrates to us his incredible love.

Allow God to minister that great love to your heart, restoring an image of deep wonder. How can you help others see the way that God sees them?

[1] Matt 2:15

BIBLE IN A YEAR: **Numbers 2,3; Acts 14**

How Should we Live?

Take a moment to be still before God. Allow the peace of the Holy Spirit to descend upon you. Let this time be precious, fuelling your day.

In today's reading, Hosea's message continues to remind the people of where they have come from and how far they have drifted from God. Rather than seeking to return to the God who had called them in the first place, they were preferring to offer peace treaties with international rivals. A key message comes in verse 6, where we read, 'But you must return to your God; maintain love and justice, and wait for your God always'. They are challenged to wait for God rather than be tempted to buy help from other nations. God does not want them to return to the land of their former slavery (Egypt), or to put their faith in the land in which they would end up being exiled (Assyria).

Sometimes the familiarity of what we have already experienced is more attractive an option than trusting God to answer our prayers, but God wants us to develop a resilience in our faith, holding fast to some of the basics like love, justice and patience. When Simon Peter failed Jesus, he returned to the comfort of the fishing boats. Part of his restoration process was declaring his love for Jesus and following him, leaving behind the old familiar practices.[1]

Some of Hosea's listeners used dishonest scales, rather than maintain justice. Some of them trusted in their wealth, as if they could buy their way out of corruption – but all areas of our lives lie open before God. Whenever we feel that faith is too hard, bring it to Jesus. The grace that helped Peter is the grace that is offered to us. Through all of this, we are reminded of the words of Micah, that we are required to 'act justly and to love mercy and to walk humbly with your God'.[2]

Consider the areas of love, justice and faith-filled patience. Are there any areas that you need God's help with today? Are there areas in which restoration is required?

[1] John 21 [2] Mic 6:8

BIBLE IN A YEAR: **Numbers 4,5; Acts 15**

Having an Eternal Hope

Holy God, we rely upon you for all things. Help us this day to trust in you, being thankful for all that you give. Lead us, we pray.

Right in the midst of a passage filled with God's righteous judgement, we read, 'Where, O death, are your plagues? Where, O grave, is your destruction?' (v 14). Paul, of course, takes these verses and encourages his readers that, through Jesus, there is a victory that transforms the mortal into the immortal.[1] The experiences we have now are not the end of the matter. For those who place their faith in God, there is a redemption that lasts into eternity.

We look backwards to Jesus' crucifixion, as we look forwards to our future hope. Hosea's listeners, however, were reminded of other works of God to inspire their hope. The trouble with their history is that it was filled with an ebb and flow of their own faithfulness. As we read in verse 6, when they were satisfied with blessings, then they turned away from God. While things are different for us who follow Jesus, it is still easy to become complacent and lose our first love. It is quite easy to slip into a consumerist approach to church and forget the grace we have received, or the mission we are all called to. Let us draw close to God in the good times as well as the hard.

As we head towards the end of Hosea's message, we must not forget that he is having to deliver this message to the people he lives with. On top of that, in some instances his life has been living out the prophetic message. The threat of God's judgement, which he continues to deliver, is peppered with hope and grace, just as Hosea himself shows to his faithless wife. Through Jesus, our message is redemption and reconciliation, all based upon the judgement of God turned upon Jesus on the cross.

Be open to the possibility that there are areas in your life that are displeasing or dishonouring to God. Bring them to Jesus, allowing him to minister redemptive grace.

[1] 1 Cor 15:55

BIBLE IN A YEAR: **Numbers 6,7; Psalms 26,27**

The Fruitful Way

Holy Spirit, may we know your promptings, hear your leadings and be open to all you have for us, that we may know the way and walk in it.

As Hosea brings God's message to its completion, we are reminded of the need to rely upon God. Throughout, we have heard that sins are punishable, but God is full of grace. Here, the people are given a big hope: as they leave idolatry behind, God will heal them and help them flourish. Many years later, when the people returned from Exile, they had given up their tendency to worship alternative gods. Through such tribulation, they were refined and, by the time Jesus came, many were expectant of the Messiah.

Jesus tells us that we cannot bear fruit unless we remain in him.[1] It is from him, the vine, that we, as branches, become fruitful. So too, Hosea's audience hear God say, 'I am like a flourishing juniper; your fruitfulness comes from me' (v 8). This image of a fruitful tree reminds us of Psalm 1, where those who are described as well-rooted trees are the blessed ones. God's choice of simile is no surprise. We can all appreciate the blessing of a fruitful tree, compared with an unfruitful one. Jesus made that clear with a fig tree![2] Fruitfulness is a sign of the kingdom of God. Although we may go through barren times, the end aim is fruitfulness.

Hosea's listeners are given the choice: walk in God's ways and be fruitful, or do your own thing and stumble. The easy thing is to make the choice to follow God: it is the subsequent journey that puts us to the test and challenges our faith and mettle. Yet, we know that 'The ways of the LORD are right' (v 9). However hard it may be, there is no better path for us to walk. After all, Jesus is 'the way and the truth and the life'.[3]

Do you know someone who is finding it hard to remain on the 'way'? Do you, or they, need a friend to help them keep to the path today?

[1] John 15:4,5 [2] Matt 21:18,19 [3] John 14:6

BIBLE IN A YEAR: **Numbers 8,9; Acts 16**

Scripture Union

FEATURES STUNNING LINE ILLUSTRATIONS FOR CHILDREN TO COLOUR IN

THE PERFECT GIVEAWAY AT YOUR EASTER EVENTS!

Just £10 for a pack of 10

Jesus Died For Me? is a poetic retelling of why Jesus died, how he rose from the dead and how he did it all for us.

BUY NOW AT: su.org.uk/Easter

DON'T GET TOO COMFORTABLE!

I suspect that few of us read the epistle from James with any frequency. As one commentator wrote, it is 'one of the forgotten books in the back of the New Testament.'[1] Part of the reason for that is, I believe, historical – as we shall see.

The author of this letter is generally considered to be the James referred to in Acts and Galatians[2] as the leader of the church in Jerusalem and the Lord's brother, who became a believer following Jesus' death and resurrection. He writes to a community of Jewish Christians living outside Israel (1:1) who are in trouble. Not only are they struggling with trials (1:2), but they are also struggling with issues of speech, wealth and poverty, favouritism, quarrelling and a general failure to behave in a way that reflects their status as followers of Jesus. They are a community that is self-deceived (1:22). James is uncompromising as he writes to correct their behaviour. As a result, this letter is immensely practical: James' aim is to highlight the behaviour expected of Christians, because 'faith by itself, if it is not accompanied by action, is dead' (2:17).

It is this last statement, I believe, that explains the neglect of this letter, because it appears at first glance to contradict Paul's teaching.[3] This is not the case, however, as the epistle challenges the Christian, saved by faith, to be whole-hearted in their subsequent devotion to God. We need Paul's teaching that faith alone saves us (how we enter God's kingdom), but we also need James' teaching that saving faith is never without consequences (how we live in that kingdom). James is not a comfortable read for many and perhaps it should not be. We all need a spiritual health-check to ensure that we are living a life of faith worked out through our actions. According to James, without such actions, our faith is dead. None of us wants that said about us!

Julie Robb

FOR FURTHER READING
C Blomberg and M Kamell, *James*, Zondervan, 2008
DP Nystrom, *James*, The NIV Application Commentary, Zondervan, 1997

---

[1] Blomberg and Kamell, *James*, 2008, p21 [2] Acts 15:13; 21:17–19; Gal 1:18,19; 2:9 [3] Rom 3:21–24

James 1:1–11

Not an Option

Spend time praying that, as we consider this letter, we will be open to the challenges God will bring to us through our reading and thoughts.

In these opening verses, James introduces some of the topics he will be addressing throughout the letter. As a result, there are a number of issues introduced and this can make James' argument in this section difficult to follow, but there is coherence if we understand that this forms the 'thematic foundation'[1] for the entire letter.

James begins by recognising that this is a community experiencing trials (v 2). The natural response to tough times is to ask questions about the source of those trials, the rationale for them and how we should respond. James is certain that the only way these questions can be properly answered is to ask for God's wisdom (v 5), given generously by God to those who ask without doubting, because to doubt God is to be 'double-minded' (vs 6–8). Introduced in verse 9, another issue that James will go on to address in the letter is the problem of rich and poor within the community and, specifically, the transitory nature of wealth and the fact that God honours the poor.

Who has not experienced tough times? James says that we should respond in joy because of what God will do in us as we go through these times. This is countercultural, because it appears nonsensical, but God is more interested in our growth in maturity (v 4). We recognise that truth requires God's wisdom precisely because the world will say it is absurd. However, that is not the only countercultural aspect of James' teaching in this passage. The value the world gives to wealth and its possession and to those who lack such wealth is turned on its head. At the beginning of James, we are reminded that we are called to live differently from the world. This is not optional!

Pray for God's wisdom to see the world as he sees it and to enable you to live differently within it. Remember, God gives generously to those who ask.

[1] Blomberg and Kamell, *James*, 2008, p22

BIBLE IN A YEAR: **Numbers 10,11; Acts 17**

Reset your Thinking!

'By perseverance the snail reached the ark.'[1]

Continuing his introduction, James returns to the issues of trials (v 12). There is an end goal to persevering through trials. Such a person is 'blessed' and promised a 'crown of life'. This beatitude tells the community that, despite their circumstances, their perseverance under trial is not a pointless exercise. There is a future hope for all those who love God.

The problem for some of us when going through trials is, of course, the temptation to blame God, questioning his goodness. James will have none of that thinking. If trials lead to sin, that is because of the 'evil desires...' within us (see v 14), which are entirely our responsibility. Note how, in verse 15, James moves from conception through birth, maturity and death. Evil desires might start small, but if they are nurtured the end result is not a future hope but a future destiny devoid of such hope.

The antidote is given in verses 16–18. Focusing on God's character helps to keep our minds fixed on the blessing that perseverance under trials will bring.

Have you ever wanted God to explain himself? We want reasons and, if we do not get them, the temptation is to blame God. This passage demands that we lose that kind of thinking, as that is to conceive an evil desire which, unchecked, grows and develops and leads to death. Rather, our focus needs to be on God's character and the goal to which we are being led. We might not be feeling 'blessed' right now, but that is exactly what James says in this passage. Contrary to the world's values, God's blessing does not mean an easy life. Countercultural living means understanding blessing with a completely different mindset. Do you need to reset your thinking about what blessing means in your life?

Paul wrote, 'Now there is in store for me the crown of righteousness'.[2] Meditate on the joy that will be yours when you receive your 'crown'.

---

[1] CH Spurgeon, 1834–92 [2] 2 Tim 4:8

BIBLE IN A YEAR: **Numbers 12–14; Psalms 28,29**

Psalm 85

Resolving Tension

'Praise be to the God and Father of our Lord Jesus Christ, who has blessed us in the heavenly realms with every spiritual blessing in Christ.'[1] Contemplate his blessings!

How much do you like living with tension? Sometimes tension is good – after all, a tug of war can only work if the rope is in tension. Nevertheless, tension is not necessarily comfortable to live with. The writer of this psalm recognises a tension that the Israelites were living within, and it is a tension that has not gone away even though we are people who live this side of the cross.

The psalmist begins by recognising how God restored his people after a period of distress caused by the Lord's anger, but brought to an end because of the Lord's forgiveness (vs 1–3). Nevertheless, the people still need restoration and forgiveness (vs 4–6). There is a tension between the past and the present. The remedy for this tension is found in God's promises and in the willingness to listen to God (v 8). Only God can resolve the tension. Only he can bring shalom and his faithful covenantal love to his people (vs 10,11). He will do what is necessary to maintain that relationship, so the psalmist can look forward to when God will restore the people and the land (v 12). Do you recognise the tension we live with? We look back to Christ's death and the forgiveness and restoration we have received from him. The problem is that, like the Israelites in this psalm, we are still people who need forgiveness and restoration. The resolution of that tension is, as the psalmist says, to listen to God and to receive his promises. He is the same covenant-keeping God who has done all that is necessary. The cross is the place where God's love, faithfulness and righteousness meet so that we can know his shalom. We are continually forgiven and restored!

Thank God for having done all that is necessary to restore your relationship with him and for his love, faithfulness and righteousness, meeting you on a daily basis.

---

[1] Eph 1:3

BIBLE IN A YEAR: **Numbers 15,16; Acts 18**

Regular Practice Required

'... what does the Lord require of you? To act justly, to love mercy and to walk humbly with your God.'[1]

If you heard me play the piano, you would be hard-pressed to believe that I had lessons for ten years. Even at the time, I was terrible at practising. Perhaps you could tell a similar story about learning a musical instrument or some other skill. We all know that to improve in any skill, practice is required.

In our reading today, it is clear that James believes that faith in Jesus has to be more than mental assent. Rather, it must be worked out in practice, specifically in the areas of speech (vs 19–21), acting on the Word heard and not being listeners only (vs 22–25) and caring for the most vulnerable in society (vs 26,27). True faith in Jesus involves not only our relationship with Jesus but also our relationship with others. The problem is that, so often in our relationships with others, we speak and get angry too quickly, listen too slowly, are prone to self-deception and, too frequently, if unintentionally, ignore the cries for justice from the vulnerable. The threefold remedy for these problems is given in verses 21, 25 and 27. Each of these requires practice, of course, and that is precisely what James expects of us.

It is true that every one of us represents work in progress. That progress cannot happen through simply affirming our faith in Jesus and his death and resurrection. Progress happens as we live out what Jesus requires of us. In other words, we need to have a faith that is practised. How are you doing at practising your faith? I hope, pray and believe that you are not like the child Julie who was not good at practising the piano, rather, that you are those who take joy in practising!

Reflect on the last week. How have you been able to practise your faith? Ask God for his help for the areas in which you struggle.

[1] Mic 6:8

BIBLE IN A YEAR: **Numbers 17–19; Acts 19**

James 2:1–13

No Discrimination Here!

'I now realise how true it is that God does not show favouritism'.[1]

Having completed his introduction, James begins to address some major problems afflicting this community. They appear to have bought into the world's values, with its emphasis on valuing people according to wealth, showing discrimination between the wealthy and the poor who enter the community. However, the mantra for the follower of Jesus has to be 'No discrimination here!'

The favouritism shown by the community is completely contrary to the gospel of Jesus Christ. Even more problematic is that those who were being favoured were actually the people who were exploiting the community and dragging them through the courts (vs 6,7). James refers the community to the law that commands love of neighbour, but we are also reminded that Jesus said that this was the second part of the greatest commandment.[2] The problem was that every time this community showed partiality, not only were they failing to keep this specific commandment, but they were actually breaking the entire Law (vs 9,10). Those who truly trust in Jesus Christ will show mercy to others and, as such, will themselves receive mercy (v 13).

We know that God is angered by the exploitation of the poor by the wealthy[3] and that favouritism has no place in the community of God's people. It would be easy to think that the challenge of this passage does not apply to us today. However, we all need to give ourselves a spiritual health check to ensure that our values match those of our Saviour and not the world. We also need to remember that neither wealth nor poverty indicates a person's spiritual state – only salvation through Jesus Christ can do this – for 'there is no other name under heaven given to mankind by which we must be saved'.[4]

Spend some time before God giving yourself a spiritual health check. What is God showing you?

[1] Acts 10:34 [2] Lev 19:18, Matt 22:37–40 [3] Eg Amos 8:4–6; Luke 18:18–30 [4] Acts 4:12

BIBLE IN A YEAR: **Numbers 20,21; Acts 20**

James 2:14–26

Not What it Seems

'Love so amazing, so divine, / demands my soul, my life, my all.'[1]

For many today this passage may be very familiar, because it is a *cause célèbre* for many Christians who affirm that salvation is by faith alone – in particular, the Pauline doctrine of justification by faith,[2] which James appears to contradict in his various statements that faith without works is dead (vs 17,20,26). Such statements might, at first sight, give credence to that idea.

However, that is to miss the fact that this passage is not divorced from the preceding verses (vs 1–13). James has not abandoned the issue of the rich and poor within the community. The question posed and answered is: 'How is true faith demonstrated?' Not by pious good wishes (vs 14–17), but by caring for the most vulnerable within the community. It is not enough, as we noted yesterday, to have a faith that mentally assents to principles. After all, Satan and his demons have no doubt of God's existence and they shudder (v 19) – but that does not lead to salvation. It is by actions that the community demonstrates its faith in God and, to justify this, James uses the examples of Abraham and Rahab to show how their faith in God was demonstrated by their actions (vs 21–25).

It is important to note here that James is not describing how one comes to faith and new life in Christ; rather, he is talking about how that faith and new life grow and mature. Scripturally, we need both: Paul and his teaching that we are saved by faith alone; and James and his teaching that true faith must also be worked out in our relationship with others. To those who would pervert Paul's teaching, James provides a rebuttal; to those who would pervert James' teaching, Paul provides a rebuttal.

Give thanks to God for your salvation by faith alone and ask him how you can show that faith in practice.

---

[1] Isaac Watts, 1674–1748, 'When I survey the wondrous cross'   [2] Eg Rom 3:21–24

BIBLE IN A YEAR: **Numbers 22,23; Psalm 30**

James 3:1–12

Sticks, Stones and Bones

'Dear Lord and Father of mankind, / forgive our foolish ways'.[1]

What can be missed about this passage, with its vivid teaching on the power of the tongue, is its context (vs 1,2): it is addressed to aspiring teachers in the community. Teachers usually make significant use of their tongues so, although this teaching is also broadened to 'anyone' (v 2, NASB), perhaps the message here is being particularly applied by James to those who would teach.

The familiar analogies in verses 3–5 emphasise the power of the tongue and the destructive impact words can have. The tongue's influence is not just confined to the impact on others, because it also has a profound influence on the person speaking the words (v 6). Regardless of the remarkable things that humans have achieved in taming wild animals, the tongue remains to be tamed (vs 7,8). Despite our best efforts, we still find that our tongue will be praising God one moment and, the very next moment, speaking words that have the potential to destroy another human (vs 9,10). James is clear that this should not be and that, just as nature can only produce what is true to its nature, so Christians should only produce words true to that nature (vs 11,12).

We all know that words can damage another and some of us have been deeply wounded by others' words. The good news is that, by the power of the Holy Spirit, these wounds can be healed and that there is forgiveness for those who recognise that their tongues have hurt another. For those in need of healing, we may need the support and prayers of someone we trust. For those who need forgiveness: have we asked Jesus to forgive – and might we need to go to another and ask for their forgiveness for the words we have used?

'May these words of my mouth ... be pleasing in your sight, LORD, my Rock and my Redeemer.'[2] This is the only remedy for the power of the tongue.

[1] JG Whittier, 1807–92 [2] Ps 19:14

BIBLE IN A YEAR: **Numbers 24,25; Acts 21**

Two Ways to Live

'Dear Lord, three things I pray: to see thee more clearly, love thee more dearly, and follow thee more nearly, day by day.'[1]

The problem with our modern Bible translations is that, in splitting chapters into sections, it is easy to lose the coherence of a chapter. In today's reading, James has remained with the context of verses 1 and 2 where he is addressing the teachers in the community. Much like the teaching on the power of the tongue, the broader category of 'anyone' (v 2) remains in view.

Two kinds of wisdom – true and false wisdom – are set before us in much the same way that Proverbs contrasts wisdom and folly.[2] James sets out the origin of these two kinds of wisdom. True wisdom originates in God; false wisdom in the 'demonic' (v 15). Each kind of wisdom is demonstrated through behaviour. False wisdom is demonstrated by those for whom self-aggrandisement is key (v 14), which ultimately leads to discord in the community. In contrast, those who show true wisdom are marked by seven attitudes (v 17) underpinned by humility (v 13). Every one of these attributes is, of course, fundamental to God's character. As we, the followers of Jesus, embrace this true wisdom, we grow in likeness to Christ and ultimately this leads to peace within the community.

Community discord or community peace – which would you prefer? We would all like to be part of a community of peace, but it can never be peace at any price. The peace referred to by James does not negate that first attribute of true wisdom – purity. True wisdom cannot find an accommodation with false wisdom, simply to maintain peace, and sometimes conflict does have to be faced. However, it takes true wisdom to know when that is required. Key to that is humility not self-aggrandisement. Which wisdom are you pursuing today?

'The fear of the Lord is the beginning of wisdom, and knowledge of the Holy One is understanding.'[3] Pray that God will help you as you pursue true wisdom.

---

[1] Richard of Chichester, 1197–1253 [2] Eg Prov 9:1–18 [3] Prov 9:10

BIBLE IN A YEAR: **Numbers 26,27; Acts 22**

James 4:1–12

Don't Fracture: Enhance!

'Follow God's example ... and live a life of love, just as Christ loved us and gave himself up for us as a fragrant offering and sacrifice to God.'[1]

Despite the chapter break, James is pursuing the same thought as in our reading yesterday, as he continues to address how the two kinds of wisdom are worked out in the community.

James describes a community that is as far from a demonstration of true wisdom as it is possible to get (vs 1–5). Discord, fights and quarrels appear to be the norm. The problem has its roots in the desire of some in the community to be friends with the world – but this is not a neutral friendship. It is a statement of one's position vis-à-vis God. James uses an Old Testament metaphor with which God castigated his people for failure to live as he commanded – the metaphor of adultery.[2] The remedy for this is given in verse 6 with a quotation from Proverbs 3:34, emphasising the humility that should characterise Christ's followers. How is that humility demonstrated?

Through 'a staccato barrage of short commands'[3] and obedience to these (vs 7–10), the believer can stop being 'double-minded' (v 8), draw near to God and see his or her life and community transformed.

Running as a thread throughout Scripture is the importance of community. That thread continues in James as he highlights the behaviour that enhances and does not fracture community life. It is true that community life is not necessarily easy. In the West, at least, we need to lose our focus on individualism and realise that we all, wherever we are located, are called to be part of a community. Community life needs to flourish. What are you doing to enhance your community life? What might you be doing that fractures the community? Look again at verses 7–10. Are you living this way?

'The Christian is saved not in isolation but as a member of the community.'[4] Pray that your life will enhance the community of which you are part.

---

[1] Eph 5:1,2 [2] Eg Hos 1–3; Isa 57:3; Ezek 16:1–34 [3] Blomberg and Kamell, *James*, p185
[4] Kallistos (Timothy) Ware, b1934

BIBLE IN A YEAR: **Numbers 28,29; Psalm 31**

Nothing is Off-Limits

'Know that the LORD is God. It is he who made us, and we are his; we are his people, the sheep of his pasture.'[1] Rejoice in being a sheep!

The psalms demonstrate that the Israelites clearly felt there was nothing off-limits with God in terms of expressing their feelings. In our psalm today, we can capture something of the desperation of the writer in the plea for rescue and the cry to God for help.

As verse 14 indicates, the psalmist is being attacked by people who arrogantly dismiss God as an irrelevance. However, the psalmist is confident that God will act precisely because of who he is – the incomparably great God before whom even the pagan nations will one day worship (vs 8–10). It is God's nature that motivates the psalmist's prayer (v 5). In times of trouble the psalmist finds comfort in God's nature and so commits to God and his service (vs 11–17), despite circumstances. Even as the psalmist pleads with God, commitment to him is renewed with the request for single-minded devotion to God (v 11). Despite challenging circumstances, the writer is confident in God, even if those circumstances challenge that confidence.

At the beginning of 2020, very few could have predicted the challenging circumstances that, as I write, many are still experiencing. The Covid-19 pandemic affected everyone reading these notes to some measure and, for some, that measure was overwhelming. The 'arrogant foes' (v 14) we faced were not human but they were no less a threat to life and I am sure we all cried out to God for his mercy. In our distress, we had no other hope but God. The emotions we felt and might still feel are not inappropriate for the faithful follower of God. This psalm illustrates that. Perhaps you need to pour out your emotions to God. After all, he is 'abounding in love to all who call to him' (v 5).

What emotions do you need to pour out to God? Nothing is off-limits. There is nothing you can say that will surprise him. Give him your honesty.

---

[1] Ps 100:3

BIBLE IN A YEAR: **Numbers 30,31; Acts 23**

James 4:13–17

Autonomy vs Sovereignty

'For I know the plans I have for you'.[1] Thank God that he has a plan for your life and that he is working it out.

In this section, James returns to the theme of money, or rather the pursuit of wealth and the temptation to plan without any reference to God.

It would appear that there was a local group of rich merchants who were making plans and presuming that they had sovereignty over their lives (v 13). Not only that, but they were boasting about the autonomy they had to act in this way (v 16). The problem was, as the merchants knew, life is transitory. James uses the metaphor of 'mist' that appears and disappears to highlight the brevity of life (v 14). The remedy for this is to recognise that all one's plans need to be brought under God's sovereignty (v 15). Of course, 'If it is the Lord's will …' could be used in a formulaic manner by Christians who simply add that to their plans, but James is using it to convince the merchants that God's sovereignty extends over all areas of their lives. Verse 17 has wider implications but, in the context of the merchants, the verse is a reference to the fact that they know how they ought to act in their business lives but do not do so. This, as James says, is sin.

If anything has demonstrated the fact that, although we can make plans, God remains sovereign, the Covid-19 pandemic has done so. All our plans had to be readjusted or abandoned as a result. It is important to stress that Christians are not forbidden from making plans, but they need to be submitted to God's will as a genuine act of surrender to the one who is sovereign. He is the Sovereign Lord who knows the 'end from the beginning'.[2] We must submit to him.

'How do you make God laugh?', so the saying goes: 'Tell him your plans!' Let's submit our plans to him, recognising the truth of 'if it is the Lord's will'.

[1] Jer 29:11 [2] Isa 46:10

BIBLE IN A YEAR: **Numbers 32,33; Acts 24**

Warning and Encouragement

'Oh, the depth of the riches of the wisdom and knowledge of God! How unsearchable his judgments, and his paths beyond tracing out!'[1] This is the God we worship!

Today's reading continues with the theme of riches or, more precisely, 'rich people' (v 1) who are oppressing the community to whom James writes – and these are roundly condemned by James. The opening verses contain, perhaps, the harshest statements within the letter, as James' accusations and warnings are uncompromising in tone (vs 1–6). How should the oppressed respond in this situation? They should wait for the coming of the Lord, because at that time God will judge those who abuse their wealth to oppress others. Just as the farmer has to wait patiently, unable to do anything to speed the growth of his crop, so those who are oppressed should wait patiently for the Lord's return, in the realisation that the timing of this is the Lord's (vs 7,8). James reminds the oppressed that the patience required is the same as that shown by the prophets and by Job, who persevered through his time of trial (vs 10,11). In the final verse of our reading today, we have the closest thing to a direct quote of Jesus within the letter.[2] In context, it seems to refer to another response that the oppressed should avoid – taking vows that signify their impatience with God's timing.

James' warning to the rich oppressors and encouragement to those being oppressed lies in the fact that the Lord will return. To those who oppress others, Jesus comes as judge. To those who are oppressed, James offers hope that, when Jesus returns, justice will be served. The warning and encouragement are as relevant today as when James wrote. We know which message is applicable to us. If it is the warning, then we need to heed it; if it is the encouragement, then take heart: Jesus is coming back! Will we be ready?

'"… I am coming soon." Amen. Come, Lord Jesus.'[3] Spend time searching your hearts so that you will be ready for his return.

[1] Rom 11:33 [2] Matt 5:34–37 [3] Rev 22:20

BIBLE IN A YEAR: **Numbers 34,35; Acts 25**

Develop your Theology

Lord Jesus, we come to you today recognising that you are God and that our only response to you is to acknowledge your greatness and our humanness.

Our final passage focuses on the topic of prayer, particularly prayer in times of sickness. The problem of sickness is an omnipresent reality and James is clear that the only approach to be taken is to pray and, where necessary, to call others to pray. These prayers, offered in faith, says James, will lead to healing (v 15) as will the confession of sin (v 16). James supports this teaching with the example of Elijah who 'prayed earnestly' (v 17), highlighting persistence in prayer.

This seems straightforward, but we know it is not quite as simple. I am sure we can all recite examples in which James' instructions have been followed but the person being prayed for has not received that healing. Great sensitivity, therefore, needs to be exercised in applying this passage. First, not all sickness is the result of sin[1] and not all sin leads to sickness. Second, our prayers are always heard but, difficult as it may be to accept, God does not always remove sickness.[2] God is not our puppet who will respond every time we pull the strings.

Prayer and healing are mysteries and none of us can provide an adequate answer to why some do not receive healing. The Western world, at least, places a high premium on eliminating anything that causes even the mildest discomfort – while at the same time some of our brothers and sisters elsewhere in the world face struggles on a daily basis that we, in the West, cannot imagine. Perhaps we need to develop a theology that allows for suffering and not just healing. Even as we do this, we can take heart that there will come a time when we will no longer require a theology of suffering or healing, because there will be no more pain, crying or death.[3]

What steps would help you to develop a theology of suffering and of healing? How might we help our communities to develop such theology?

[1] See John 9:1–3 [2] Eg Paul in 2 Cor 12:7–10 [3] Rev 21:4

BIBLE IN A YEAR: **Numbers 36; Deuteronomy 1; Psalm 32**

THE LORD'S WAY OF LOVING

The prophet Jonah was advisor to the evil King Jeroboam II of Israel.[1] Jonah's prophecy about the extension of Israel's borders had come true – a national victory for Israel and a personal triumph for Jonah! Now, however, Jonah receives an unexpected and unpalatable assignment: 'Go' to Nineveh and 'preach against it' (1:2). Nineveh was the capital city of the mighty and merciless Assyrians – an ancient Near Eastern superpower – and its destruction would have greatly strengthened Israel's national security. Jonah shared the national zeal 'that tried to make God the exclusive property of Israel, refusing to accept the universality of God's grace.'[2] God's warnings of judgement typically included 'grace periods' within which people could repent (see 4:2).[3] Jonah ran away because he did *not* want the Ninevites to repent and be spared destruction.

The focus in Jonah, unlike other prophetic books, is not the *message* but the *messenger*. Jonah is not a sermon but a story of God's undiscriminating grace, extended equally to the rebellious Ninevites and to his reluctant prophet Jonah – representing Israel, who had also shirked its mission to bless the nations. Jonah 1 and 2 depict the prophet's wilful defiance; Jonah 3 and 4 describe his resentful compliance. Jonah's attitudes are mirrored in the two sons in Jesus' parable.[4] Initially, he behaves like the younger: rebellious, running away, learning through harsh experiences, before gratefully receiving grace. Later, his behaviour resembles the older son, outwardly obedient yet inwardly resentful and resistant to giving grace. As Philip Yancey wrote in *What's so Amazing about Grace*,[5] 'Jesus did not give the parables to teach us how to live [but] to correct our notions about who God is and who God loves.' Jonah's story serves the same purpose. In his poem 'Coming Around',[6] Thomas Carlisle depicts Jonah waiting for God 'to come around to his way of thinking', while God waits for Jonah and for *all* of us to 'come around to his way of loving'!

Tanya Ferdinandusz

FOR FURTHER READING
DW Baker, D Alexander and BK Waltke, *Obadiah, Jonah, Micah*, Tyndale Old Testament Commentaries, IVP, 1988

[1] 2 Kings 14:23-25 [2] *Dictionary of Biblical Imagery*, IVP, 1998 [3] Jer 18:7,8 [4] Luke 15:11-32 [5] Zondervan, 1997, p53 [6] In *You! Jonah!*, Eerdmans, 1968, p64

Jonah 1:1–16

Running

'Where can I go from your Spirit? Where can I flee from your presence?'[1] How does this thought comfort you? Or make you uncomfortable?

The book of Jonah begins with the customary formula of prophetic books: 'The word of the LORD came to Jonah' (v 1). Two verses later, the story takes off in an unexpected direction when Jonah takes off towards Tarshish in the west instead of heading east to Nineveh (v 3).

Jonah flees from 'the presence of the LORD' (vs 3,10, NRSV) – but it is unthinkable that this prophet, who professes faith in the all-powerful Creator (v 9), would have imagined he could escape from God's presence! Desmond Alexander suggests that 'by fleeing from the Lord's presence Jonah announces emphatically his unwillingness to serve God'.[2] Jonah isn't running from God's *presence* so much as refusing to serve his *purposes*. Under Jeroboam, the extension of Israel's borders had protected Israel's national interests. Since this happened 'in accordance with the word of the LORD ... spoken through

his servant Jonah',[3] it would also have furthered Jonah's career as a prophet. Should we conclude that Jonah was prepared to serve God's purposes only so long as this furthered his own? Even the unbelieving sailors are appalled by Jonah's disobedience. Their outraged 'What have you done?' (v 10) echoes God's question to Eve after humanity's rebellion in Eden.[4] These sailors seem to be more sensitive to the things of God than God's own prophet (vs 6,14,16)! As Jonah runs, God relentlessly pursues, ready to move heaven and earth – and literally moving wind and waves (vs 4,11)! – to reach his runaway prophet. A great wind is 'hurled' upon the sea, cargo is 'hurled' overboard, Jonah is 'hurled' into the sea (vs 4,5,15, ESV). All this hurling and raging is like a wrestling match between God and Jonah! Unlike Jacob, who wrestled with God because he yearned for God's blessing,[5] Jonah wrestles with God's desire to bless Israel's enemies.

Are you running from God? How might he be pursuing you? Will you let him catch you?

---

[1] Ps 139:7 [2] In Baker, Alexander and Waltke, *Obadiah, Jonah and Micah*, TOTC, IVP, 1988, p101 [3] 2 Kings 14:25 [4] Gen 3:13 [5] Gen 32:22–30

BIBLE IN A YEAR: **Deuteronomy 2,3; Acts 26**

Repenting?

'If I go up to the heavens, you are there; if I make my bed in the depths, you are there.'[1] How has God met you, in highs and lows?

Contrary to popular belief, SOS, recognised as an international distress signal since 1908, is not an abbreviation for 'Save Our Ship' or 'Save Our Souls' – although these terms may seem appropriate, since it *has* saved many ships and lives![2] In chapter 1, God had saved a ship from being wrecked and he provided a huge fish to save Jonah from drowning (v 17). From within the belly of the fish, Jonah gratefully recalls how God had responded to his SOS (v 2).

Jonah's running from God is depicted as a gradual going 'down': *down* to Joppa, *down* into a Tarshish-bound ship, then *down* to the lowest part of the ship.[3] Now, going lower still, he 'sank down' to the ocean bed (v 6). When you hit rock bottom, the only way is up! Sensing that 'life was ebbing away', Jonah 'remembered' God and sent up a distress signal (v 7). Was Jonah's SOS a despairing cry to save his *skin* or a contrite plea to save his *soul*? Jonah's prayer (vs 2–9) contains acknowledgement of his hopeless plight and gratitude for God's salvation, but does it demonstrate real repentance?

Medieval theologians distinguished between *attrition* (sorrow over sin due to fear of God's punishment) and *contrition* (sorrow over sin because it has grieved a loving God). Although Jonah declares that 'Those who cling to worthless idols forfeit God's love for them' (v 8), he fails to confess that he himself had turned away from God's command. He sees 'specks' in other eyes while ignoring the 'plank' in his own![4] Despite vows to offer 'grateful praise' and 'sacrifice' (v 9), there is no confession of sin, no expression of contrition, no commitment to change. Jonah affirms that 'salvation comes from the LORD' (v 9), but he still grudges the Ninevites God's salvation.[5]

Evaluate the graciousness and generosity of your grace-giving against the benchmark of God's grace in your life. How do you rate?

[1] Ps 139:8 [2] https://en.wikipedia.org/wiki/SOS [3] Jonah 1:3,5, NKJV [4] Matt 7:3 [5] See Jonah 4:1–4

BIBLE IN A YEAR: **Deuteronomy 4,5; Acts 27**

Responding

'... you perceive my thoughts from afar ... Before a word is on my tongue you, Lord, know it completely.'[1] How do you feel about being known so completely and comprehensively?

God's Word comes to Jonah again, representing a second chance (v 1). Having *rescued* Jonah from death,[2] God now *reinstates* him in his prophetic role (v 2) – like Peter's recommissioning following his denial of Jesus.[3] From defiance, Jonah has graduated to compliance (v 3). But what is the state of his heart? Minimum-wage legislation safeguards employees against exploitation, but these laws are not intended to discourage employers from paying just and generous wages. Jonah's sermon is brief, even brusque (v 4). He says nothing about who God is or how God loves;[4] he doesn't try to persuade the Ninevites to repent; he doesn't share his own powerful testimony of God's grace. Jonah's 'minimum wage' brand of sermon fails to reflect the 'maximum mercy' quality of God's grace! Unfolding events will reveal that, although Jonah tweaked his behaviour, he had not experienced the change of heart that characterises genuine repentance.[5]

Although the messenger remains unmoved, 'The Ninevites believed God' (v 5). Much scholarly ink has been spilt in debating the authenticity of their response. Nevertheless, the text confirms that the Ninevites didn't merely perform rituals of repentance (vs 5,6,8a) but also 'turned from their evil ways' (vs 8b,10a) – in stark contrast to Jonah, whose outward obedience (v 3) is not matched by a turning away from sinful prejudices. Clearly, God took the Ninevites' repentance seriously, since he turned from 'his fierce anger' (v 9) and 'relented' from his decision to destroy Nineveh (v 10).[6] This does not, however, mean that Nineveh experienced lasting revival; this story relates only to the response of this particular generation of Ninevites.[7]

'... the eyes of the Lord range throughout the earth to strengthen those whose hearts are fully committed to him.'[8] What will the Lord see in *your* heart?

[1] Ps 139:2,4 [2] Jonah 2 [3] John 21:15–19 [4] Jonah 4:2 [5] Jonah 4 [6] Cf Matt 12:41 [7] See the book of Nahum [8] 2 Chr 16:9

BIBLE IN A YEAR: **Deuteronomy 6,7; Psalm 33**

Citizens of God's City

'We're citizens of high heaven! We're waiting the arrival of the Saviour, the Master, Jesus Christ'.[1] Praise God for the privilege and hope of your heavenly citizenship.

A city on a hill attracts attention because of its elevated location. God's city was founded on Mount Zion. The reason 'Glorious things' were said of this city was that God himself dwelt there among his people (vs 1–3). Israel was inclined to interpret this special relationship narrowly, selfishly, arrogantly, enjoying the benefits and blessings of being chosen while ignoring God's mandate to bless 'all peoples on earth'.[2] Jonah, for example, wanted the Assyrians excluded – even exterminated! – and resented God's 'concern for the great city of Nineveh'.[3]

The psalm continues with an unexpected prophecy: Rahab (Egypt), Babylon, Philistia, Tyre and Cush will also enjoy citizenship in God's city! These nations were enemies and oppressors of God's people; yet, here is God promising that he will treat them as if they were 'born in Zion' and include their names in the registry of his people (v 4). Membership in God's family or citizenship in God's kingdom is not conferred on any of us as a birthright but can only be received as a gift, by faith: 'to those who believed in his name, he gave the right to become children of God ... born of God'.[4] Jesus' love embraces *all* people, not just those who accept him but even those who oppose him. Our good shepherd relentlessly pursues 'other sheep that are not of this sheepfold' so that he may 'bring them also' into the fold.[5] This is how we, who are privileged to be counted among his sheep, must view those on the outside – not as enemies who are excluded but as those who must be warmly, urgently, persuasively and lovingly invited so that they, too, might be included among the inhabitants of God's city.

'You're here to be light ... God is not a secret to be kept. We're going public with this, as public as a city on a hill.'[6]

[1] Phil 3:20, *The Message* [2] Gen 12:3 [3] Jonah 4:11 [4] John 1:12,13 [5] John 10:16 [6] Matt 5:14, *The Message*

BIBLE IN A YEAR: **Deuteronomy 8,9; Acts 28**

Jonah 4

Resenting

'Search me, God, and know my heart; test me and know my anxious thoughts. See if there is any offensive way in me, and lead me in the way everlasting.'[1]

In Jewish tradition, Jonah is read on Yom Kippur (the Day of Atonement) – a celebration of the matchless mercy of God, a God who Jonah knows is 'sheer grace and mercy, not easily angered, rich in love, and ready at the drop of a hat to turn your plans of punishment into a programme of forgiveness!' (v 2, *The Message*). Despite knowing God's character and having been a grateful beneficiary of God's gracious salvation,[2] Jonah reacts with angry arrogance (vs 1,3,4,9) when this same undeserved grace is extended to his enemies. Jonah is impatient with God's patience. Still wrestling with faulty notions about who God should love, Jonah resents the fact that God 'relents' (v 2).

The God who is 'slow to anger' (v 2) confronts Jonah's anger: 'Is it right for you to be angry?' (vs 4,9). While God's anger rises up in right judgement against evil, his justice is always tempered by compassion and a loving concern for all his creatures (vs 2,11).[3] 'The language of God's judgement must be heard through the agony of God's heart.'[4] Jonah's anger, however, is sparked by self-centredness and narrow nationalistic concerns.

Jonah's prediction came true. God turned his plans of punishment into a programme of forgiveness because the Ninevites, despite rebelling against God's *laws*, had repented of their evil ways.[5] But Jonah has *also* rebelled – against God's *love*. Will he repent and come around to God's way of loving? Like Jesus' parable of the lost son,[6] Jonah's story ends on an inconclusive note: 'should I not have concern for the great city of Nineveh …?' (v 11). The reader is not told how Jonah responded, perhaps because God's searching question addresses not just Jonah, not just Israel, but *every* believer in *every* generation. How will *you* reply?

Lord, you search me and know my heart. Now help me to know your heart, so that my living and loving are in step with your heartbeat.

[1] Ps 139:23,24 [2] Jonah 2 [3] Also Jonah 3:9,10 [4] Christopher JH Wright, *The Message of Jeremiah*, IVP, 2014, p97 [5] Jonah 3:10 [6] Luke 15:11–32

BIBLE IN A YEAR: **Deuteronomy 10,11; Romans 1**

GOD'S DIVINE PLAN

This last section of the Gospel of Luke focuses on the final week of the life of Jesus as he embraced his destiny. This is the end of his earthly life and ministry, as he was betrayed, crucified and then rose again. As Jesus entered Jerusalem as king, the crowd shouted jubilantly, while the religious leaders rejected him. Looking beyond the exterior beauty of the Temple, Jesus saw that the true worship of God had been abandoned. Because of this, he wept, leading to the cleansing of the Temple and the prediction of its destruction. Religious corruption during the time of Jesus was not only restricted to the Jerusalem Temple. As we take time to examine our own temples, where God dwells, we may find things that need to be cleansed from them, too.

The religious leaders had been relentlessly trying to trap and kill Jesus. They found an insider, one of Jesus' disciples, who was willing to betray him, thus paving the way for Jesus' crucifixion. As dark as the night may seem, however, we must not forget that death does not have the final say. On Easter Sunday, Jesus rose from the dead. The women who went to the tomb, the two disciples on the road to Emmaus and the eleven disciples, to whom Jesus appeared, were all sceptics of the resurrection who needed to move from doubt to faith. The Gospel of Luke places repeated emphasis on the fact that the Messiah must suffer, die and rise again in fulfilment of the Scriptures (9:22,44; 18:31–33; 24:7,26,27,46–47). This is part of the divine plan of salvation. Without the cross, there is no gospel. The Gospel of Luke ends by inviting us to be witnesses of this gospel, where 'repentance for the forgiveness of sins will be preached in his name to all nations' (24:47). We have a message to share!

Kar Yong Lim

Luke 19:28–44

Unexpected Triumph

'Open my lips, Lord, and my mouth will declare your praise.'[1]

When my parents were alive, we travelled to our home town annually as part of our tradition, celebrating the Chinese Lunar New Year. There was great excitement during our journey. The pilgrims of old were no different. Each year, they journeyed to Jerusalem for the Passover celebration as required by the Law of Moses.[2] For Jesus and his followers, their feeling of tiredness after a long and weary journey would have given way to a sense of joy and excitement as they descended the Mount of Olives. Here they were greeted by a panoramic view of Jerusalem and the majestic Temple. Israel's long-anticipated Messiah and King entered Jerusalem riding on a colt, as a fulfilment of Zechariah's prophecy.[3] The crowd journeying with Jesus shouted joyfully, 'Blessed is the king who comes in the name of the Lord!' (v 38). Yet there was a dark cloud hanging over this whole incident.

The religious leaders did not receive their king (vs 41–44). Instead, they wanted to quash the excitement and silence the praises of the people (v 39). Jerusalem had rejected her Messiah and the Temple had abandoned the true worship of God. That was enough for Jesus to weep for the city. Israel had headed down a road that did not lead to peace (v 42) but to destruction. As a result, Jesus predicted the destruction of the Temple for forsaking God (vs 43,44).

The world we live in today is no different from the Jerusalem who rejected its king. In many parts of the world, hostility towards the Christian faith is rising. In some countries, church attendance is declining and many are abandoning the faith. Do we weep for our nation, city, or even our church? Will we stand in the gap and pray for our nation and church?

O Lord, look with mercy upon us according to your steadfast love. Have mercy on us and our nation.

---

[1] Ps 51:15 [2] Deut 16:16 [3] Zech 9:9,10

BIBLE IN A YEAR: **Deuteronomy 12–14; Romans 2**

Cleansing the Temple

'... true worshippers will worship the Father in the Spirit and in truth, for they are the kind of worshippers the Father seeks.'[1]

I was awestruck when I first visited St Paul's Cathedral in London. There is a sense of majesty in the architecture that draws me to worship God. In the first century, every pilgrim to Jerusalem would have been deeply impressed by the Temple, the spiritual centre for the Jews and the pride of the nation. However, Jesus was not concerned with the exterior beauty of the Temple. He had wept over the city (vs 41–44). Now, he was about to do something unimaginable. When Jesus entered the Temple, he kicked up a commotion by driving out those who were trading there.

The Temple was the heart of Israel since its foundation was laid during the days of Solomon. Sadly, over the years, the Temple had been corrupted to the point where true worship of God was diminishing. Decades before the first Temple was razed to the ground by the Babylonians, the prophet Jeremiah had warned the people about their false trust in the Temple, denouncing their evil acts of injustice, oppression and idolatry.[2] God declared that the Temple had become 'a den of robbers'[3] where he was robbed of his worship. This same passage was cited when Jesus cleansed the Temple. He was denouncing exactly what Jeremiah did – the acts of injustice and oppression present in the Temple of his day.

Jesus would not let such corruption draw people away from true faith and worship of God. Imagine Jesus visiting our churches today. Would he be pleased with what he saw on the inside? Would he cleanse your church? What about our body as the temple of God? What would Jesus find inside our hearts?

Lord, strengthen the hands that serve, the ears that hear and the feet that go where you send them, that we may do justice, love kindness and walk humbly with you.

[1] John 4:23 [2] Jer 7:1–29 [3] Jer 7:11

BIBLE IN A YEAR: **Deuteronomy 15,16; Psalm 34**

Power of Storytelling

'Create in me a pure heart, O God, and renew a steadfast spirit within me.'[1]

Jesus is a great storyteller. His stories teach us about the kingdom of God[2] and he also uses them to respond to the religious leaders. After witnessing him cleansing the Temple and seeing him teach there, the chief priests, scribes and elders confronted Jesus by questioning his authority to do such things (v 2). The hostility towards Jesus had been escalating since he entered Jerusalem, to the extent that the religious leaders had plotted to kill him.[3] Here, Jesus responds to the religious authorities by asking them whether the source of John the Baptist's authority was God or not (vs 3,4). Placed in a dilemma, the religious leaders refused to answer (vs 5–8). Jesus continued by telling the story of the vineyard owner and his tenants to state his point.

Through this parable, Jesus made it clear that the religious leaders had failed to submit themselves to God's rule. He also exposed what was deep within their hearts. They were self-centred. Their wilful disobedience and stubbornness had blinded them to the work of God. As a result, horrible consequences awaited them. The Temple was not too far from destruction when the most important part of the building, the cornerstone, was rejected. This was fulfilled in AD 70, when the Romans destroyed the Temple.

The religious leaders certainly did not fail to understand what Jesus was saying. They plotted, for the second time since Jesus entered Jerusalem, how they might lay hold of him (v 19).[4] Their ultimate rejection of Jesus would soon climax in his crucifixion.[5] In our Christian discipleship, have we been like the religious leaders when we intentionally ignored God's voice speaking to us through his Word? Will we be willing to repent of our ways and seek God for forgiveness?

'Today, if you hear his voice, do not harden your hearts.'[6]

[1] Ps 51:10 [2] Luke 8:1–18; 13:18–21 [3] Luke 19:47,48 [4] See also Luke 19:47 [5] Luke 23:26–49 [6] Heb 4:7

BIBLE IN A YEAR: **Deuteronomy 17,18; Romans 3**

What Belongs to God?

'Know that the Lord is God. It is he who made us, and we are his; we are his people, the sheep of his pasture.'[1]

The religious leaders did not show any sign of slowing down their attacks on Jesus. They decided to use another method to trap him. They asked Jesus whether one should pay taxes to Caesar. If he were to reply in the negative, this was tantamount to sedition and the Roman authorities could arrest him. If he said yes, the religious leaders would then discredit him, as many viewed this tax as oppressive and were not in favour of paying anything to Caesar. Jesus avoided the dilemma by asking about the image found on the coin. When the religious leaders replied that it had the image of Caesar, Jesus said, 'Then give back to Caesar what is Caesar's, and to God what is God's' (v 25).

Jesus' reply is not meant to be the final say about the relationship between the state and the church. It is to remind us that what is legally due to the state in various forms of taxes cannot be avoided by any responsible citizens. However, we must always bear in mind that Caesar's rights are limited. He has no rights in God's domain. When his boundaries encroach into our obedience and devotion to God, we must take a stand. The believers in the early church responded with a firm statement, 'We must obey God rather than human beings!'[2]

This is a reminder for those of us who live as a minority in some parts of the world. There may be restrictions imposed on the practice and propagation of the Christian faith. Wisdom is needed so that we can live as faithful Christians. We must always remember that our life belongs ultimately to God, and we should never bow our knee to any Caesars in our life. We give our life, faith, worship and obedience to God himself only.

'Fear the Lord your God, serve him only.'[3]

---

[1] Ps 100:3 [2] Acts 5:29 [3] Deut 6:13

BIBLE IN A YEAR: **Deuteronomy 19,20; Romans 4**

Luke 20:27–44

Trick Question

'See what great love the Father has lavished on us, that we should be called children of God!'[1]

One of the religious groups during the time of Jesus, the Sadducees, did not believe in the resurrection. It was their turn to entrap Jesus as the conflict with him intensified. They crafted an absurd question about the wife of seven men through levirate marriage and hoped to refute the belief in the resurrection held both by Jesus and by the Pharisees.[2] The law of levirate marriage states that if a man dies childless his brother will marry his widow and raise their children, in the name of the deceased brother. This is to ensure that the line of descent is kept.[3]

In their question, the Sadducees gave an example of a man who died childless. Then his brother married the widow but also died childless, and this continued until the seventh brother who married the widow and remained childless. Then the widow died. Whose wife would she be since she had married so many men? The Sadducees thought that they could embarrass Jesus by firing their best theological shot. Jesus refuted them by saying that in the resurrection life, there is no more marriage. There is no need to be bothered about preserving one's family line.

Jesus' answer is important. It is an affirmation of what we recite in the Nicene Creed: 'We look for the resurrection of the dead and the life of the world to come'. In our world today, where there are doubts about resurrection and a rising belief in reincarnation, we are reminded that death is not the end for us. What happens beyond death hinges on one's response to Jesus. We should not worry which man is the husband of the widow. Instead, we should be concerned whether we are children of God.

'Yet to all who did receive him, to those who believed in his name, he gave the right to become children of God ... born of God.'[4]

---

[1] 1 John 3:1 [2] Acts 23:8 [3] Deut 25:5,6 [4] John 1:12,13

BIBLE IN A YEAR: **Deuteronomy 21,22; Psalm 35**

The Silence of God

'Wait for the LORD; be strong and take heart and wait for the LORD.'[1]

Globally, we are going through one of the most difficult periods we can remember with the Covid-19 pandemic. The challenges we face in our workplaces, churches and homes are unprecedented. Many colleagues and loved ones succumbed to the attack of the virus. I have attended more funerals in these few years than in the previous decade. One of the most difficult issues raised is that we feel that God seems to be silent in these challenging situations. It leaves us feeling forgotten and rejected.

The psalmist in our reading today had gone through an extremely difficult situation. He expresses his feelings of being depressed, forgotten, grieved, outcast and terrified. The range of emotions we read about in Psalm 88 can be overwhelming. In his cry to God, he wonders if God is ever present.

The ending of the psalm is probably the most depressing: 'darkness is my closest friend' (v 18). It is not surprising that this psalm is acknowledged as the saddest psalm of lament.

However, the psalmist's hope is found not in its ending but in its beginning: 'LORD, you are the God who saves me; day and night I cry out to you' (v 1). Before he pours out his lament and gives a long list of things that have gone wrong in his life, the psalmist declares his hope in the Lord, even through his experiences of the dark night of the soul and the silence of God. Throughout this psalm, he continues to cry out to God repeatedly (vs 1,2,9,13), not to any other gods or persons. The psalmist has the quiet confidence that God hears him. His dark seasons in life do not mean that God is absent, but rather how much he desperately needs God.

Remember that in the darkness of life, we need God even more. We can always believe his promise that he will never leave nor forsake us.

---

[1] Ps 27:14

BIBLE IN A YEAR: **Deuteronomy 23,24; Romans 5**

Luke 20:45 – 21:4

Beware of External Piety

'Search me, God, and know my heart; test me and know my anxious thoughts.'[1]

Fresh from responding to the challenges set by the religious authorities (vs 1–44), Jesus turned his attention to the disciples. He warned them about teachers of the Law. They were concerned with their outward appearance, trying to win approval from people, yet they were hypocritical in their religious behaviour. Instead of demonstrating care, concern and compassion for the needy, they took away the houses of widows, the most defenceless people of the day. Because of this despicable act, Jesus declared that they would be judged (v 47). The teachers of the Law become the example the disciples should avoid. Instead, they are to follow the attitude of the widow who came into the Temple and gave to God two copper coins, the smallest currency of the day.

The lesson we should take from the story of the widow is that what matters is not the amount one gives but the amount that one keeps for oneself. The rich gave out of their abundance and they still had much left for themselves. However, the widow gave all she had. That was real sacrifice. She became an example of one who was rich towards God, who sought first the kingdom of God and who was willing to give up everything in her devotion to God.[2]

The world we live in encourages us to pay attention to our outward appearance. The fashion industry, cosmetic and beauty products, aesthetic and cosmetic surgery are all billion-dollar business. While we take care of how we present ourselves to the world, let us care also how we appear before God and how we live our lives. Let us learn from the widow how we may seek the kingdom of God and guard our hearts from external piety that could only earn us the praises from people.

'The Lord does not look at the things human beings look at. People look at the outward appearance, but the Lord looks at the heart.'[3]

---

[1] Ps 139:23 [2] See Luke 12:21-34 [3] 1 Sam 16:7, TNIV

BIBLE IN A YEAR: **Deuteronomy 25,26; Romans 6**

Destruction of the Temple

Outward beauty may please our eyes, but inner beauty shines brightest.

The Eiffel Tower in Paris, Big Ben in London and the Petronas Twin Towers of Kuala Lumpur are examples of city symbols today. In the first century, the Temple of Jerusalem was the icon of the city. Every pilgrim to Jerusalem was deeply impressed by it. However, Jesus was not impressed by what he saw there. On the day after he entered Jerusalem, he cleansed the Temple.[1] Later on, the disciples commented about the beauty of the Temple, leading Jesus to predict its destruction (v 6).

The destruction of the first Temple by the Babylonians was etched in the culture of the Jews in the first century. None of them could comprehend how God would allow this to happen again. Jesus then explained to the disciples the signs of when the Temple might be destroyed (vs 8–24). There would be false prophets, wars and persecution (vs 9–18). The exhortation to 'Watch out' and 'Stand firm' (vs 8,19) emphasises how much Jesus wanted the disciples to be prepared for the disaster and not to be caught unawares and be led astray.

In AD 70, the Temple was destroyed by the Roman armies. Today, on the western edge of the platform of the Temple, huge stones that were thrown down during the destruction are still visible – truly 'not one stone will be left on another; every one of them will be thrown down' (v 6).

The warnings of Jesus speak to us today. As we look at the external beauty of our lives, we may think that all is well with us but, if we are honest with ourselves as we take a hard look deep within, what will we find? Are we like those religious leaders during the time of Jesus who refused to repent of their sins? Or are we prepared to keep watch and stand firm at all times?

May we examine our lives so that we will not drop our guard and be complacent.

[1] Luke 19:45,46

BIBLE IN A YEAR: **Deuteronomy 27,28; Romans 7**

Luke 21:25–38

Prepare for his Coming

'Lo! He comes with clouds descending'.[1]

After predicting the destruction of the Temple, Jesus continued his conversation with the disciples by shifting the focus to his second coming. It is important in this discourse to note two warnings given by Jesus. The first involves a warning to be on guard so that we are not overcome with drunken revelry and concerns of this life. The second warning is to be alert and pray at all times. Only by heeding these warnings will we be prepared for the day of Christ's coming and not be caught unawares (vs 34,36). Instead of addressing when the destruction of the Temple and his coming would take place, Jesus drew the attention of the disciples to their own readiness.

The recent Covid-19 pandemic has resulted in increased interest in end-times prophecies in some Christian circles, with some trying to predict when the second coming of Jesus might take place. Our reading today reminds us that we should not be speculating when the end of time might come. What is central to the teaching of Jesus is for us to keep watch and be ready at all times. We should live our lives in the light of his coming again! We should not be like those caught unprepared – as with the flood in Noah's day and Sodom's destruction in Abraham's time.

How can we be watchful today as we patiently wait for Jesus' second coming? What must you change and what must you do differently, as you live your life in light of Jesus' coming again?

O Lord, make us watchful and awake as we await your coming, that when you appear you may find us faithful in your service and joyful in hope.

[1] Charles Wesley, 1707–88

BIBLE IN A YEAR: **Deuteronomy 29,30; Psalm 36**

Plotting for Betrayal

'Dear friend, do not imitate what is evil but what is good.'[1]

The passion narrative[2] begins with the plot of the religious leaders to kill Jesus during the Passover celebration. Their earlier attempts were unsuccessful because of the crowd.[3] They needed another scheme to get rid of Jesus. Judas became the solution, after Satan entered him. He agreed, with the exchange of money, to help the religious leaders get hold of Jesus in the absence of the crowd.

The Gospel of Luke is explicit in revealing Satan as the driving force behind Jesus' betrayal. The passage does not explain what may have led Judas to do this. What is important is that Satan is portrayed as having his way and he seems to be triumphing. Earlier in his earthly life, Jesus had encountered Satan in his temptation.[4] At the end of Jesus' temptation, Satan left him until

an 'opportune' time.[5] That moment had arrived: Satan entered Judas, leading to the arrest, trial and crucifixion of Jesus. Yet, as dark as the night may seem, we must not forget that evil does not have the final say. The emphasis of the Gospel of Luke is that the death of Jesus is the heart of the divine plan of salvation. It is repeatedly mentioned in Scripture that the Messiah must suffer and rise again.[6]

We see so much evil in our world today. The rise of injustice, wars, killing of innocents and the displacement of people are some of the troubling news stories confronting us on a daily basis. While we may feel helpless, we must not lose hope. The days of evil are numbered. God will put things right. Let us be vigilant as we wait patiently for the return of Christ to rule and reign.

'Hate what is evil; cling to what is good.'[7]

[1] 3 John 11 [2] Luke 22:1 – 23:56 [3] Luke 19:47,48; 20:19 [4] Luke 4:1-12 [5] Luke 4:13 [6] Luke 9:22,44; 18:31-33; 24:7,26,27,46,47 [7] Rom 12:9

BIBLE IN A YEAR: **Deuteronomy 31,32; Romans 8**

Luke 22:14–23

The Last Supper

'Then Jesus declared, "I am the bread of life. Whoever comes to me will never go hungry, and whoever believes in me will never be thirsty."'[1]

Passover was a major festival observed by the Jews to commemorate God's deliverance of his people from slavery in Egypt.[2] During the period of the New Testament, this celebration generally involved the practice of drinking four cups of wine with the meal and recalling God's earlier promises.[3]

During the meal, on this occasion, Jesus took the bread, broke it and gave it to the disciples. In breaking the bread, he was reinterpreting the meaning of the bread to refer to his body and the cup to refer to his blood poured out for many (vs 19,20). This signifies that Jesus intended this meal to be celebrated after his death and resurrection in remembrance of him, just like the Passover meal was observed by the Israelites to remember the deliverance of God. Significantly, Jesus also mentioned that he would not eat the meal (v 16) nor drink the fruit of the vine until the kingdom comes (v 18). He was indicating that the entire creation is still patiently waiting for this day when we will celebrate the heavenly banquet. Then, God will take people from every tribe and nation as his own. There is a strong eschatological significance in the participation in the last supper.

As we participate in Communion, we not only look back to the finished work of Jesus on the cross but also forward, to his coming again. We recall the words of Paul: 'For whenever you eat this bread and drink this cup, you proclaim the Lord's death until he comes.'[4] May we be ready for the second coming of Jesus.

O Lord, as we celebrate this memorial of breaking the bread and drinking the cup, may we be faithful to proclaim Christ's death until he comes.

---

[1] John 6:35 [2] Exod 12,13 [3] Exod 6:6,7 [4] 1 Cor 11:26

BIBLE IN A YEAR: **Deuteronomy 33,34; Romans 9**